CAPACITY-BUILDING FOR COMMUNITY ORGANISATIONS

idasa

This publication was made possible through support provided by the Office of Democracy and Governance, Bureau for South Africa, U.S. Agency for International Development, under the terms of Award No. 674-A-00-03-00015-02. The opinions expressed herein are those of the author(s) and do not necessarily reflect the views of the U.S. Agency for International Development.

ISBN 1-920118-48-9

Published by the Institute for Democracy in
South Africa (IDASA)
Cnr Prinsloo and Visagie Streets
P.O Box 56950
Arcadia 0007
Pretoria
South Africa

Website: www.idasa.org

Editing: Jo Tyler
Design: Valerie Phipps-Smith
Cover design: Jo Tyler

CONTENTS

COMMUNITY ORGANISING

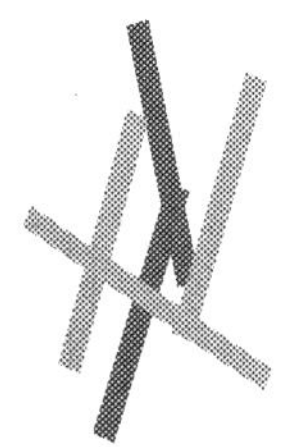

1. Introduction

The single most powerful asset that community-based organisations (CBOs) have is that they are so close to the people in their communities.

This means you and your organisation are best placed to identify the needs of your community. You also are most able to organise the different sections or parts of your community in a way that ensures their voices are heard and they have a say in what happens in the community.

This notebook will guide you on some of the strategies and techniques you can use to enable your organisation to have the biggest impact possible at a local level. You might use some of these strategies and techniques already. The main aim of this guide is to help you to check to see if what you are doing can be improved by using the structured tools and techniques of development. We hope that you will find some new ideas that will make your work at local level more powerful.

It is important to note that when people talk about community-organising in the field of development, they are usually trying to sensitise and show development workers in outside organisations how to be respectful of communities. This is knowledge that you and your community have already and you have probably discussed this with people working in your community.

However, sometimes those of us who work in CBOs might make some of the same mistakes that outside agencies make. This notebook is a guide to help those who work in your organisation to learn from the mistakes that many of these agencies make. In many ways the issues raised in this guide will serve only as a reminder for the people who volunteer or work for your organisation to ensure that it is the community which drives your programmes and projects.

The main objective of community-organising is to improve local governance so that the lives of people at a grass-roots level are improved. Effective community-organising can and must transform fundamentally how governance takes place.

It should empower members of communities to drive the development agenda in their communities. It also should enable citizens to hold accountable structures of government, as well as outside development agencies.

The notebook will examine what we mean by community-organising, the difference between community-mobilisation and community-organising, the steps that should be followed when mobilising and the different aspects that will ensure community organisers are effective. It also will highlight areas of concern that should be addressed during the organising process.

2. Definitions and models

2.1. What is community?

The word community is used all the time by people working in development. It is assumed that everyone knows what we mean when we say 'the community wants something' or 'this is in the interests of the community'. It is useful to stop sometimes to examine what we mean when we use the word 'community'.

Traditionally a community is a geographical place, which can refer to a village, town, district, city or refugee camp. But communities also can be groups of people organised around interests. For example, you could refer to a community of HIV activists, a community of police officers, a community of small business owners or a community of brick builders.

To see if a group of people are a community, you should ask these questions:

- Is there a sense of belonging by the people in the community?
- Is there a common purpose and common goals among the people of this community?
- Do the people in this group define themselves as being part of a community?
- Is there co-operation between the members of the community?

Often the word 'community' is used to label a large group of people. However, even within large communities there might be smaller communities that operate separately. Within a township community, for example, there might be smaller communities, such as the Muslim community, or communities that are made up of young women, disabled children or cultural associations.

It will be easier to organise if you and your organisation are clear about which part of the community you need to work with to achieve your aims.

The word 'community' is used often to describe all the people in a certain area. However, often there are divisions between the people who make up that community. These divisions might be because of economics, religious beliefs, tribal differences or age differences. The differences also might arise because people cannot agree on how to achieve certain goals.It is important to take any tension among community members into account when you are planning to organise any action.

You might have to build a sense of community with others so that you and your organisation can work collectively to organise citizens. In all communities there are some people who have organised themselves into groups already. However, you might find that there are many people who are not organised, but who would like to be. Often it is the poor and most marginalised in a community – such as children running households affected by HIV/AIDS – who you can help so that they can learn to organise themselves.

This example might help you to understand the concept. Ashley is a thirty-something woman who lives in a small mixed-income suburb in Durban. The picture below represents her community.

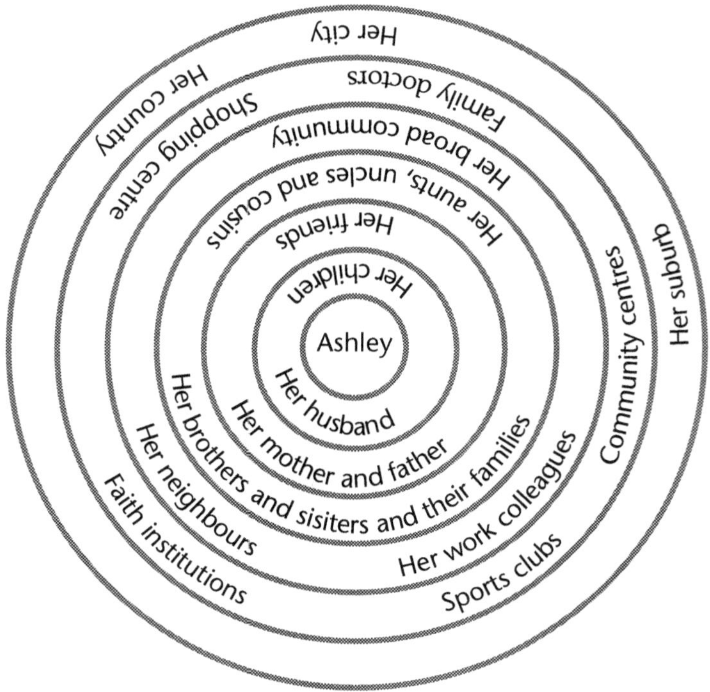

This kind of illustration is known as a community onion. To get the full picture of a community, think of it as made up of layers like an onion. Just as you find many different layers in an onion, a community is similar: there are many different layers and many different people and organisations that make up that community.

Communities are places where people work together to achieve common goals. Usually CBOs are created for a certain purpose. To be effective the technique of community-mobilisation can help your community.

2.2. What is community-organising?

Community-organising is bringing people together to achieve a goal.

Various role players need to take action to achieve the goal. The role players should come from all walks of life, including people from formal organisations, community leaders and individual citizens.

Community participation should be sustainable and ensure that decision-making processes at a local level are transparent and accountable to individual citizens and organisations. It also should make the community more self-reliant so that it can sustain a better lifestyle for all who make up that community.

Citizens often feel disempowered on a social, psychological and/or political level in their community, which is why it is necessary to organise people. Through social organising political power can be restored to communities, enabling them to change their environment and improve their standard of living.

2.3. Organising vs mobilising

Mobilising is usually associated with protest politics. In South Africa, particularly in the last decades of the apartheid regime, leaders of the struggle worked tirelessly to mobilise communities. At that point in South Africa's history, the strategy of mobilising the masses was extremely effective. The government began to see the extent of people's anger and realised that support for overthrowing apartheid was overwhelming. After the unbannings and the 1994 elections a conscious effort was made to 'demobilise' communities.

Mobilising strategies allow for mass participation and, because of this, they can be said to be democratic. However, they are not the most effective strategies for building the capacity of citizens. Leaders tend to remain firmly in control. They decide on any action, sometimes in a consultative manner, if the situation allows, and sometimes not. Then they mobilise citizens to support it. Actions include marches, mass meetings, boycotts, strikes, etc. The work of mobilising mainly involves persuading people to swell the numbers. Citizens on the ground are not involved in planning the action itself – they simply follow orders. During the action, the leaders have the highest visibility, addressing meetings and speaking to the press.

By contrast, the work of **community-organising** focuses on development. **The golden rule of organising is: 'Do not do for others what they can do for themselves.'** This is often a difficult rule for leaders to follow. They fall into the trap of thinking that they need to 'rescue' communities. Often leaders believe that they have all the answers and that communities should pay attention to their ideas. A community organiser begins by listening to people, not by telling them what to do. Organising is based on respect for the history, traditions and knowledge of communities.

Organising strategies rely on building public relationships. Conducting interviews provides a tool for strengthening these relationships. Organisers are motivated by the fundamental belief that citizens have talent, energy and resourcefulness. Community-organising is about liberating this potential. In particular, the organiser consciously works to develop people's public skills and confidence, enabling them to speak in public, meet authorities, evaluate actions and demand accountability.

Organising work goes beyond protest. It is attentive to diverse interests and aims to bring different groups together to solve problems. Above all, organising is not coercive. It does not strive to drum up massive support in the shortest possible time. It is slow, patient work. People become involved in an action not because of emotional appeals or instructions to do so, but because they make a personal commitment on the basis of their own self interest in that action. A community organiser is a catalyst, aiming not for personal visibility, but striving to build people's capacity to speak on their own behalf and to initiate action themselves.

Sometimes organising and mobilising work overlaps. Each situation determines the best strategy. The main difference, however, is in where the most power lies – with the leaders or with the people. Mobilising tends to use command and control, while organising emphasises collective action, shared power and capacity-building.

2.4. Assumptions and principles

The assumptions that underlie community-organising can be summarised as follows:

- Problems are experienced collectively;
- People (including those who might have otherwise been 'labelled' as vulnerable) are highly resourceful and the process aims to maximise these resources;
- These community resources are supplemented, only if necessary and appropriate, by selected external resources;
- The community defines its own needs and objectives;
- Planning and decision-making are the responsibility of the community and occur in a bottom-up rather than top-down manner;
- The interests of the community as a whole take priority over those of individuals;
- Participation is a key concept; and
- People must 'own' whatever project is undertaken so that it reflects the community's cultures and values and ensure its sustainability.

The **principles** of community-organising are:

Capacity-building

As an organiser, primarily your job is to build the capacity of the individuals in the community so that they become active citizens rather than having to rely on you or outsiders for community action.

Social responsibility

At all times, as an organiser, you are responsible in your community. All actions taken have consequences and you should think these through.

Transparency and accountability

Just as one of your aims is to ensure that governance is an open process, so too is it important that you are transparent and accountable in your community. You should ensure the community knows about decisions and processes that your organisation undertakes.

Sustainability

This is probably the most difficult of all the principles. You must ensure that all initiatives are sustainable and can be grown and maintained. This applies to all resources, not only financial resources.

Gender equality

Our Constitution makes provision for the principle of gender equality. This is sometimes difficult because often people are committed to the old-fashioned ways of operating in society. This might mean that men believe they are the decision-makers and women also might believe that men are the key players in making decisions in the community.

Research has shown, however, that if you empower the women in any community the likelihood of success is much greater.

Do no harm

When organising in your community, your actions should improve the lives of the people. You should not cause any harm. If, for example, you create tension between different groups that cooperated effectively before, you have done harm to the community.

You should keep these principles in mind in each of your tasks and in all your actions.

2.5. The role of CBOs in the community

As a CBO in your community your role is to:

- Help people to organise themselves, clarify ideas on needs and objectives and of ways to achieve them. You need to be the catalyst in the community;
- Help to facilitate representative leadership and democratic structures;
- Provide knowledge and information;
- Provide or advocate for resources to support your community's own efforts and to supplement (but not replace) their own resources. These might include training.

2.6. Community-organising model

Opposite is an illustration of the different aspects of community-organising.

3. Prepare to organise!

3.1. Knowing your community

The first step is to ensure that everyone on your team knows the community equally well. It might be useful to spend a day getting everyone to share their knowledge of the community, finding out who their networks are and who they believe has power in the community. Team members should share information on the social organisation, culture, economy, languages, layout, politics, ecology and problems in the community.

To do this most effectively you might want to draw a map of your community using the following tool:

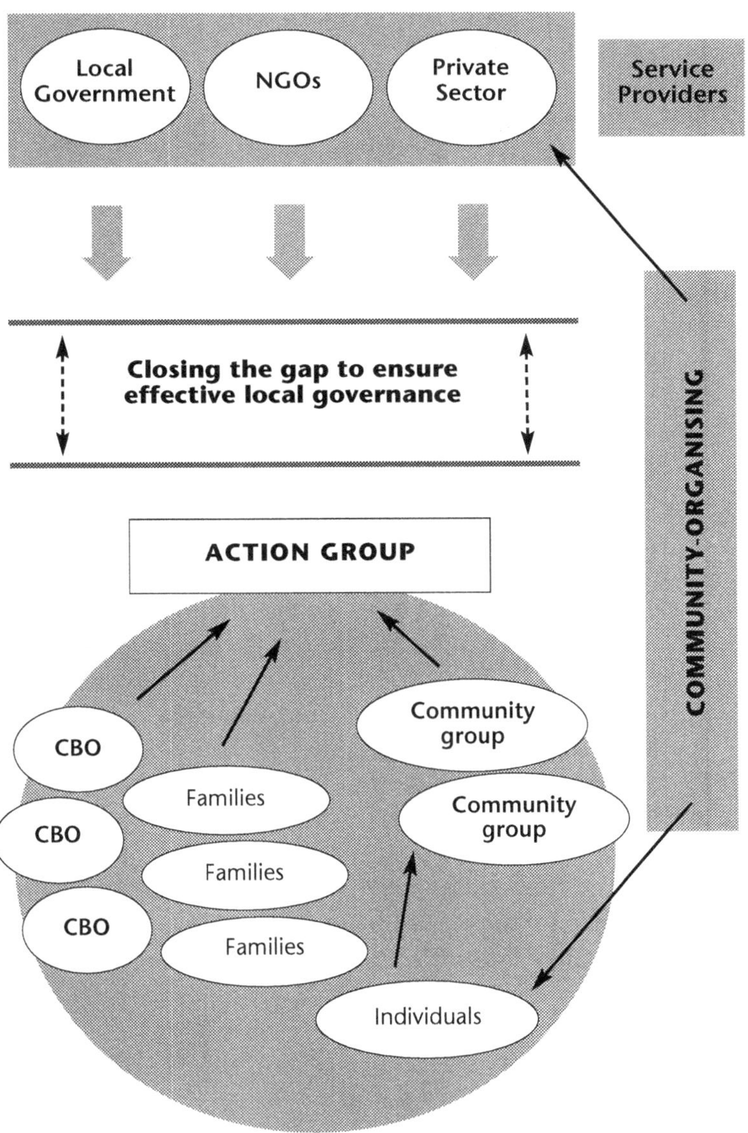

(Adapted from IFSP model)

Mapping community structures – REFLECT trainers' tool

You will need the following to construct the map:

- Flipchart paper;
- Marker pens;
- Flashcards (different colours); and
- Prestik or masking tape.

Step 1:

- After listing all the community structures, ask your team members to write them down on flash cards. They should use only one card for each structure.
- On a bigger flashcard write the word 'community' and stick it in the middle of the flipchart paper.
    - Ask your team members where in the community the structures are placed; and
    - Ask your team members if there are structures outside the community that could help you with the issue around which you are trying to organise.

After this chart is complete ask these questions:

1. What structures exist in the community?
2. What membership do they have?
3. What do they do – what is their main purpose?
4. Who do they serve?
5. How did they come together?
6. When were they established?
7. What have these structures achieved? What are the successes and challenges of each structure?
8. What do they do for the community?
9. Do they have any sub-projects running in the structure?
10. How can they be contacted? Who is the contact person? (Name, telephone, address.)

11. Who is sponsoring the structures?
12. What printed materials are being produced by these organisations?
13. How are women represented in these organisations? Do they participate? If the answer is no, ask why not. If the answer is yes, ask what roles they play in the structures.

Think Box

Team members must also continue to analyse how the different elements in their community relate to one another. A community is not merely a collection of individuals, but is a system that is bigger than individual citizens. As a system it has various aspects such as the technological, economic, political, institutional, ideological and the perceptual. People come in and go out of the community, by birth, death and migration, but the system continues. And it is always changing. Your team members need to understand the system so they can nudge ongoing change in certain directions.

It is useful to establish what kind of contact individuals have, as well as the kinds of contacts they have with local-level political decision-makers.

3.2. Knowing your goals

As a team leader you need to ensure that all the members of your team are clear about the goals of organising the community on an issue. This is critical because it is easy to get side-tracked from your goals. Team members might be running from one meeting to another; they might get involved in certain activities and could lose sight of the ultimate aim, which is to organise community members to become responsible citizens who will hold local government structures accountable for development in the community. Citizens can be organised into groups that are self-sustaining, so that they do not rely only on your organisation to help them.

3.3. Knowing the team

It is important for all members of the team to share their skills and to discuss areas about which they do not feel confident. This will help you to choose the right person for the right job.

Each member of the team should share their skills. It is important that you and your team do not abuse skills for your own interests, but use them instead for the benefit of the community. Some of the skills you need in your team are:

- Public-speaking – in a facilitative style, not a lecturing or preaching style;
- Planning;
- Managing;
- Observing;
- Analysing;
- Writing;
- Listening; and
- Conflict resolution.

These skills are discussed in some of the other notebooks in this series. It will help your team to work through these together. Remember that the best way to become good at a skill is to practise it. You can go to many courses or read many books, but you need to implement these skills on a day-to-day basis.

Characteristics that your team members will need are:

- Honesty;

- Enthusiasm;
- Positive outlook;
- Tolerance;
- Patience;
- Motivation; and
- Openness to ongoing learning.

3.4. Knowledge

Team members should have some basic knowledge of community-working concepts. This knowledge can be found in newspapers, magazines and books or by attending college or university courses.

If, for example, you want to strengthen or empower a low-income community, you have to understand why it's so poor. If your aim is to eradicate poverty, you need to know more than simply the symptoms and consequences of poverty. You will need to understand the causes of poverty so you can support and promote changes that will counteract those causes. You should realise that poverty alleviation merely reduces the pain temporarily, but does not contribute to poverty eradication.

Poverty is not merely a question of money, and money alone will not eradicate poverty. (Adapted from www.iccsa.org)

You should encourage the people in your team to keep a notebook in which they record who they talk to every day during your organising campaign. These contacts could be very useful and might give you new ideas. The notebooks will become valuable knowledge in your organising efforts in your community.

3.5. Outside resources

You might find there are donor agencies which would support your work. There also might be bigger organisations, like non-governmental organisations (NGOs), which could help you in your organising efforts.

There are advantages to getting outside help, such as access to money and other resources. But there are disadvantages too. Your efforts could go unnoticed and your achievements and goals might get swallowed up by the bigger organisations.

The biggest disadvantage is that long-term solutions are not found. Even though it is much harder to get resources from your community, it is better for the community in the long term. Resources in the community are more constant and reliable once you have identified them. Resources from outside organisations are temporary usually and cannot be relied on. For example, an outside organisation might give you money to enable you to hold meetings in the best venue in your community. But, when the organisation stops the funding, you have to meet in the school hall. It would be more constructive for both your organisation and the community to always meet in the school hall and to use money from the outside agency to improve the facilities at the school.

4. Organising your community!

Once you and your team are organised and you are clear about your roles, your implementation plan and your resources, you can begin your interactions with the rest of your community to organise them around your issue.

You should have a list of the people you need to contact to begin organising. Divide your team and give each member responsibility for contacting people and organisations from your list.

For example, you might decide that the informal settlement where you live needs a community clinic. You will need to meet people and organisations in your community who are concerned about and involved in health issues. This might include community-based care organisations, youth organisations, faith-based institutions, and nurses and doctors in your community.

4.1. Situational analysis

You need to draw up a 'situational analysis'. You might need to do some research. For example, you should find out how many people in your community have to travel long distances to access basic health care. Research the demographics of your community: how many old people there are, how many pregnant mothers there are, etc. This information will support your argument. When you meet stakeholders you should ask them if they can give you any information.

Once you have all the information, you will discover what the priority needs are in the community. For example, dental care might not be as important or necessary to the citizens as HIV/AIDS treatment.

You should ask stakeholders what kind of action they would be prepared to take. Some might be prepared to talk to politicians; others might prefer to do a door-to-door survey to find out what health services are most needed in the community.

4.2. Plan of action

Once you have all the information and the commitment of people and structures, you will need to put together an action plan. Look at the *Project Management* notebook in this series for guidance on how to put together an effective action plan.

Your plan should have the following elements:

- Detailed tasks should be laid out;
- Responsible people must be allocated to the tasks;

- Measurable objectives must be put in place to ensure that targets are met;
- Timely changes must be made to ensure targets can be met;
- You need to stick to the budget and ensure that it is well controlled; and
- You must allocate the correct equipment and materials when and where necessary throughout the project.

4.3. The organising cycle

This diagram shows the steps you need to follow when organising your community:

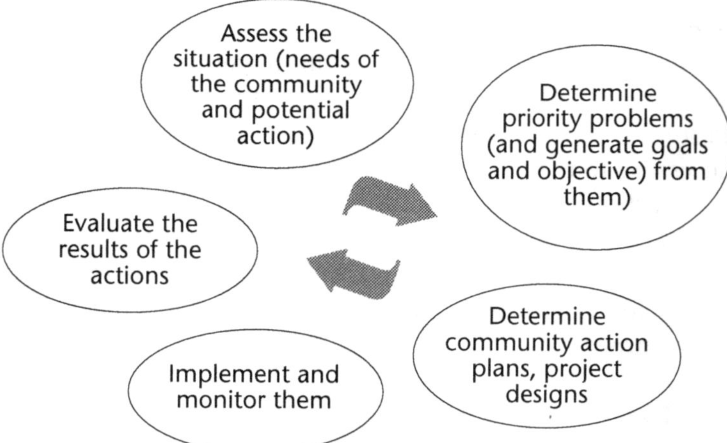

4.4. Raising awareness

When you encourage community members to organise themselves and take action you need to ensure that they are aware of the reality of the situation. Avoid raising false expectations and actively counteract the inevitable assumptions and rumours about the kind of help to expect. This means you also must be realistic.

For example, just because your community needs a clinic immediately, don't expect the government to provide one. You might need to think creatively to find ways to get the clinic. Perhaps you can approach doctors and nurses to donate their time for free. Or maybe a church will allow you to use its hall for a clinic. You might have to hold a fundraising event to get money to buy equipment and medication. You might be able to approach a pharmaceutical company to donate medicines and other medical equipment.

Explain to community members that if they remain passive and expect help from the government or from other outsiders, the community will remain poor and weak. No community is totally poor. As long as there are humans in the community there will be resources and potential.

4.5. Open dialogue

To achieve your goals you might need to use different techniques when approaching community members, such as holding brainstorming sessions, open dialogues and meetings to discuss and decide on the priority issues. You need to ensure that people are working together on a project for the right reasons, otherwise the project could flop.

You might have to challenge community members about their perceptions, their stated needs and priorities. For example, some people might support your goal to get a community clinic just because they want a bigger clinic than the community 10km away. This would not be a good reason for organising around an issue. The need for a clinic in your community must be genuine.

4.6. Challenge the community

If, while you are in the process of organising the community, you discover that it does not actually need a clinic, but would benefit more from a programme focusing on hygiene issues which could prevent an outbreak of infections, you will need to adjust your goals. Ultimately it is the biggest needs of the community that should determine the issues around which you want to organise.

Your main aim will probably be to empower the community to take charge of its own development programme. The community might have decided to build a road. But there are many different ways to build a road. You and the community have to decide on the best method that will contribute to community empowerment and effective local governance in the long term. Your CBO should help community members understand that they need take charge of their own destiny and not leave it all up to government. If you wait for the government to act, it will lead to much frustration. However, if community members are empowered and work in partnership with local government, they are more likely to get roads built in a shorter space of time.

4.7. Strengthen the community

Your CBO should ensure that it is well informed. There might be a lack of skills in your community, which could prove to be obstacles that could stop you from achieving your goals. You might not have to go outside your community to look for the necessary skills. Rather find out about existing skills programmes.

There are many skills training programmes that are run through the Sector Education Training Authorities (SETAs). Get as much information as you can about these to help strengthen your community.

Some of these training programmes will include skills that will help to build strong organisations, as well as skills such as plumbing or brick-building.

There might be people in the community who are skilled already. They could be approached to teach and mentor others.

Ongoing community meetings and information flow is critical, because these will ensure that individual members of the community feel a sense of ownership. The meetings will enable community members to raise any concerns they might have and to offer ideas and come up with suggestions to solve problems.

By ensuring community members feel they 'own' the project, you will help to sustain it. You need to get people involved so that they feel empowered and are part of the project. In the clinic example, to get citizens involved, you could ask for volunteers from the community to help with housekeeping, drawing up a medical roster, managing the office, looking for new resources, continuing to lobby the government for support for the clinic and managing any money that might come in through the fees charged for health services.

If you look at the notebooks on *Project Management* and *Strategic Planning*, you will realise that the road to achieving your goal is not always smooth. You might need to study and follow the 'organising cycle' again and again.

You also will be able to get ideas from the *Fundraising* notebook to help you get financial resources to get your project up and running.

5. One-issue organising vs long-term organising

The strategies you use to organise one urgent concern in your community will be different to those you will use to organise issues that might take time to resolve.

An example of a single issue could be speeding. Perhaps there is a road in your community where people often get hurt because of speeding. Community members might be keen to ask local government to put in place speed bumps, so that the traffic slows down and the road is made safer. You should speak to every person who has been hurt by the speeding cars; you could set up a meeting with the ward committee and the councillor in the area; and you could also involve local newspapers in covering the story.

An example of a long-term organising issue might be a plan to get housing for every person in the community. You will have to research the issue to find out how many people need housing. You also should find out whether they need single-quarter housing or family housing. You need information on what the budget for housing is at a local level and at a provincial level. You should find out if the public works department is involved and whether there will be enough schools and community facilities for the new development. You should identify locations that could be turned into housing. For example, there might be a school that has few learners and is in the process of being shut down by the education department and might be used to develop a housing project.

All communities grow constantly, so the housing project will probably not be a once-off effort. You need to ensure that your organising on the issue is effectively maintained.

To achieve your long-term goal you will have to organise meetings with many different people and organisations. You need to ensure that residents can articulate their needs. You might have to facilitate negotiations between residents and the council on the size of the development. There will be numerous tasks that need to be organised and undertaken.

Before you begin planning how to respond to a need of the community you should consider whether you are organising a single issue or a long-term issue.

6. Special interest groups

Special interest groups you might find in a community include:

- Women;
- Youth (including child-headed households);
- Disabled;
- Refugees;
- Elderly people; and
- Different faith-based institutions (such as traditional African churches, Christian churches, Shuls, Temples, Mosques, Buddhist Centres etc.)

Some special interest groups will need more organising than others. For example, if you want to organise health issues for a group of street children you will probably have to put in more effort and work than you would if you had to organise the health needs of pensioners, who might be members of structures such as *stokvels* already.

All communities have many different groups in them. Some are more wealthy than others. Some have more disabled people. Some have commercial sex workers as well as committed Christians who might not always agree on solutions to a problem.

Your job in organising the community is to help various parts of the community to identify their common interests and work together to achieve those interests. The more people with different interests who participate in the project, the better the outcome of your goals will be.

Make sure you provide enough time for the different people and organisations in the community to reach consensus. This can be a tricky process and you will need to hone your facilitation skills.

Your CBO should not be seen to side with any particular part of the community. Your task is to organise around common principles and, therefore, you should work hard to find out what the commonalities between people are and help them to focus on those, rather than on their differences.

7. Areas of concern

Many of the concerns in community organising work have been raised throughout this document. The main issue, however, that should be remembered at all times is that community organisers are facilitators. This can become difficult when you are working in the community in which you live. If you want to make an input as a member of the community you should first tell people that you are 'taking off your community organiser-cum-facilitator hat' and that you are speaking as a member of the community in this instance. Community members should always be at the forefront of the organising process.

Another concern is burnout; to avoid burnout don't work too many hours a day. It is important to be committed, but it is also necessary to lead a balanced life so that you can remain an asset to your community.

You must remember at all times that the aim of community organising is to build self-reliance among members of the community so that they do not stay dependent on outside organisations and can be in charge of their own destiny.

Pay attention to ways of keeping the community interested and on how to expand the number of people involved in the organising process. It might be helpful to team up with other CBOs in your community.

8. Conclusion

Organised communities are the heartbeat of good democracies. They ensure that between elections politicians and officials are held accountable and that they keep the promises they made during election campaigns.

Democracy is only as good as the active people who make up communities. Your organisation can make a difference by ensuring that the liberation struggle in South Africa was not in vain.

Community-organising requires commitment and patience. Mistakes will be made, but you need to ensure that the community is committed, self-reliant and able to resolve the many problems that might arise.

Different communities will have different concerns, but the principles and tools of community-organising are the same in any community. Every community needs to build and develop an active citizenry.

In societies where the citizens are not well organised, democracy is fragile and can result in leaders not being held accountable to their citizens. The more people are involved at a local governance level, the more people will realise how important democracy is in our everyday lives.

This notebook is a tool to help you to strengthen the active and democratic traditions in your community. It highlights the basic areas of community-organising. However, as with all skills, the more they are practised the easier they become. Your organisation can play a vital role in ensuring that democracy grows from strength to strength in your society.

9. References

Books

Fisher, R. 1984. *Let the People Decide: Neighbourhood Organisation in America*. Twayne Publishers. Boston.

Robinson, D. 2002. *Building Social Capital*. Institute of Policy Studies, Victoria University. Wellington.

Slim, H. and Thompson, 1993. P. *Listening for a Change: Oral Testimony and Development*. Panos Publications Limited. London.

Weisbord, R.W. and Janoff, S. 1995. *Future Search: An Action Guide to Finding Common Ground in Organizations and Communities*. Berret-Koehler Publishers, Inc. San Francisco.

Manuals

Leadership Manual. 2004. IDASA. Pretoria

Websites

http://www.icssa.org Accessed on 7 December 2005.
http://www.ifsp.org Accessed on 8 December 2005.
http://www.savethechildren.org Accessed on 8 December 2005.

COMMUNITY-BASED ORGANISATION MANAGEMENT

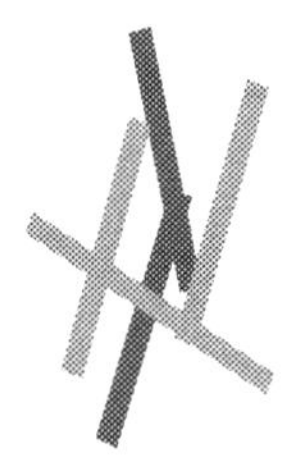

1. Introduction

Community-based organisations (CBOs) play an important and relevant role in providing services at the local level. They work in a variety of different fields, such as education, health, the rights of the disabled, gender issues, etc. Wise management of the organisation can contribute significantly to ensuring the effectiveness of the work that it does.

This notebook will provide basic and comprehensive definitions of what organisations are, what a CBO is and what management is. The definitions will help you to understand the concept of CBO management.

To fully understand the concept, the notebook will highlight management skills, different types of managers and the main functions of managers.

It also will examine different topics that need to be managed to ensure the effectiveness of the organisation, such as tasks, time, meetings, human resources, employee performance, etc.

This notebook aims to give an overview of CBO management. It should be considered only as a guideline. For a more detailed study of CBO management, it is recommended that you look at other sources, such as books, magazines, websites, and attend formal and informal courses.

You also could approach CBO managers to learn more about their practical experiences of managing their organisations.

2. What is an organisation?

An organisation is made up of a group of people who come together to accomplish a common goal or a set of goals. The size of an organisation can vary from two people to thousands of people.

Organisations can range from profit-driven companies, such as Shoprite/Checkers, to non-profit organisations, such as the Institute for Democracy in South Africa (IDASA), community youth clubs, church groups or even a book club.

The principles of management have been learnt and established over time and can be applied to all organisations, though there might be some circumstances that are specific to certain organisations. For example, the circumstances relating to management of a CBO might be quite different to those relating to management of a profit-driven company.

A key aspect that should be considered is the goal of the organisation. The goal can be explicit (recognised) or implicit (unrecognised). If you are clear about your organisation's goal, all management strategies, techniques and processes can work together to achieve that goal. Although covered in detail in another notebook in this series, it is important to note that strategic planning is useful because it can help to clarify your organisation's goals. We will highlight a few strategic planning aspects in this notebook.

It is critical that senior managers, as well as other members of the management team, understand the following aspects:

Vision

Is the image that members of the organisation have about how it should work.

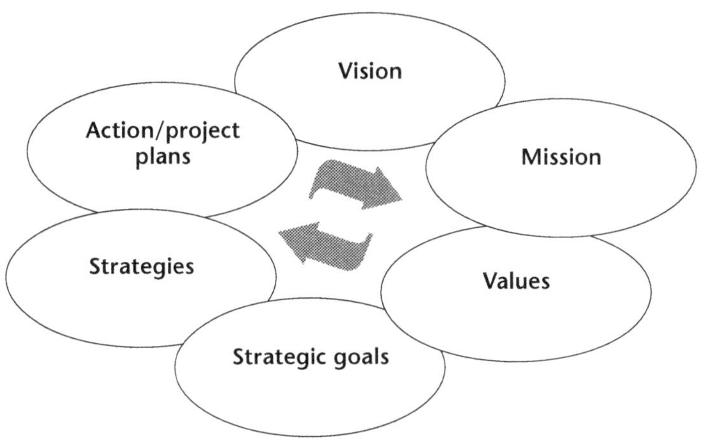

Mission
Is the overall purpose according to which an organisation operates.

Values
Are the priorities in the nature of how the organisation should carry out its activities. These values are the personality or culture of the organisation.

Strategic goals
The organisation's members must have strategic goals to work towards to achieve the overall accomplishment of the mission.

Strategies
Are the different approaches used by organisations to achieve their goals.

Action/project plans
Actions or project plans identify activities and assign responsibilities.

If managers are not clear about all the aspects of an organisation, they will not be able to lead its other members. The goals of the organisation will not be met and many people might become frustrated and disillusioned.

The focus of this notebook is management, specifically for CBOs. We will start with what CBOs are and how they differ from other types of organisations, such as government departments.

2.1. What is a community-based organisation (CBO)?

A CBO is an organisation that provides social services at the local level. It is a non-profit organisation whose activities are based primarily on volunteer efforts. This means that CBOs depend heavily on voluntary contributions for labour, material and financial support.

Characteristics of a CBO

- It is non-profit;
- It relies on voluntary contributions;
- It acts at the local level; and
- It is service-oriented.

3. What is management?

The term management has different interpretations. The most traditional is that management comprises a set of duties, such as planning, organising, leading and coordinating activities, and it also can include the group of people involved in these activities.

Management focuses on leadership skills, such as establishing the vision of the organisation and its goals, communicating these and guiding others to accomplish them. It asserts that leadership must be facilitative, participative and empowering to ensure visions and goals are established and communicated.

Management also can be understood as the group of people responsible for making decisions in an organisation, such as executives and managers. In a non-profit organisation management can be identified as members of the board, the executive director and programme directors.

3.1. Types of managers

There are three basic types of managers:

- Top managers are those able to interpret the policy of the organisation;
- Middle managers are responsible for the implementation of policy; and
- First-line managers are those who conduct routine administration.

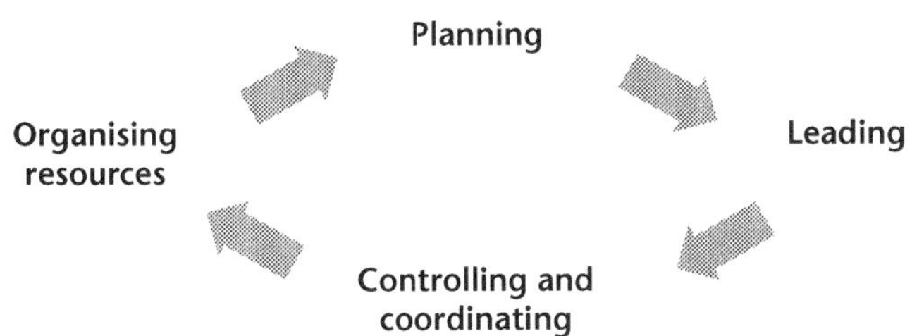

3.2. What are the functions of the manager?

The manager's functions include:

Planning

Includes identifying:

- Goals;
- Objectives;
- Methods;

- Resources needed to carry out methods;
- Responsibilities; and
- Dates for the completion of tasks.

Organising resources

This ensures that minimum resources are spent to achieve the maximum effect of the goals. This is a critical function, because all the other functions cannot take place without at least some resources being in place. Resources are not only financial, but also include people and materials.

Leading

A leader sets direction for individuals, groups and the organisation. A leader should be able to influence others and inspire them to achieve the goals of the organisation. Leadership is an aspect of management. However, you might find some good managers who might not be able to inspire others, but who are good at helping the members of their team to meet deadlines and achieve results. Some leaders also might not be good managers. It is important to find a balance between these two aspects when managing an organisation.

Controlling and coordinating

The manager needs to ensure that all the organisational systems, processes and structures are controlled so that goals and objectives can be met.

4. Management skills

We have mentioned already that management is a conscious process. Managers must always keep in mind 'the big picture' of the organisation: the needs of their departments, projects or programmes, as well as the practical day-to-day business of making sure goals are met.

To achieve this balance it is important for all managers to improve their skills constantly. Everyone – including managers – benefit from further training because it enables better performance throughout the organisation. Managers should consider the skills they have, if they need more skills, whether they are implementing the skills they have learnt and how they can improve their ability to manage even further.

We will provide a brief overview of the skills that are useful for managers. If you take management of your organisation seriously, you should read newspapers and magazines, surf websites and look at books for new information on management. Each year hundreds of new publications are brought out to guide the manager to improve his/her skills and abilities.

4.1. Problem-solving and decision-making

An important part of a manager's job is to solve problems and make decisions. Most, if not all, issues can be resolved in this way. The basic steps are:

Define the problem

You need to understand exactly what the problem is. If it seems complex, try to break down all the elements of the problem to get a clear definition of what it is and what the issues are that make up the problem.

Prioritise the problems

If there are several related problems, it is important to decide which one should be addressed first. List the problems to help you decide. Ask yourself:

- What is urgent?
- What is necessary?
- What is urgent and necessary?

The priority problems are those that are urgent and necessary.

Understand your role

The manager cannot solve all problems. Sometimes s/he needs to do only a small aspect of the work to solve the problem. A common mistake many managers make is to think that it is their job to get involved in all the steps in solving a problem. It is up to the manager to decide what can be done by others involved in the problem to help solve it.

Identify causes

Examine the potential causes of the problem. Start by describing the the problem. Ask yourself:

- What is happening?
- Where is it happening?
- When did it happen?
- How did it happen?
- Who was involved?
- Why did it happen?

Identify alternatives and select an approach

Usually there is more than one way to solve a problem. A useful approach is to brainstorm the problem, allowing input from all parties. This will enable you to choose the most effective option to solve the problem. However, do not get frustrated if you cannot solve the problem first time. Complicated issues sometimes take many attempts by all parties to be resolved.

Plan the implementation of your approach

It is not enough simply to identify an approach to resolve the problem. You must develop a plan of action and evaluate it constantly to check you are doing all you need to do to solve the problem.

Monitor and verify

All plans need to be monitored. This is particularly important if other people are involved in solving the problem. If you do not actively monitor the implementation of the plan to solve the problem, it might not get resolved. Once the problem has been resolved, you will need to verify with others to establish that they also think the problem has been resolved.

Remember that for effective decision-making the objective should be clearly defined. The manager must ensure there is sufficient information and then identify the feasible options. Once the options have been evaluated, a decision can be made.

4.2. Planning

Planning is a process that involves decision-making on the organisation (ends), the objectives (means), on how they are conducted (policies) and on the results (outcomes). This is a major management process and involves defining the ends, means, conduct and results of every step of the plan.

During the planning process the aims and objectives of an organisation might have to be redefined to ensure they are successful. The manner in which the plans are conducted also is important.

The standard planning process includes:

- The establishment of overall goals;
- The establishment of smaller goals or objectives associated with the main goals;
- The design of strategies or methods to meet the goals and objectives; and

- Identification of what resources will be needed, including how and when the methods will be implemented.

The different kinds of planning that a manager should think about are:

Short-term planning	**Medium term planning**	**Long-term planning**
Short-term plans might last from six months to a year, depending on the size of the organisation and its operations.	Medium-term plans might last from about six months to three years, depending on the organisation's size and operations.	Long-term plans might last from five to 20 years, depending on the organisation's size and its operations.

4.3. Delegation

Delegation is the art of handing over responsibility and authority to other people – often subordinates – to complete a task and allowing them to figure out how best to accomplish that task. By delegating a task to a subordinate, you are giving them the opportunity to become more developed, fulfilled and productive people. For delegation of duties to be successful, consider the following:

- Delegate the whole task to the same person: it gives him/her responsibility and increases motivation;
- Select the right person: the task should be assigned to someone who has appropriate skills and capabilities;
- Clearly specify the expected results: all the relevant information – who, what, how, where, why – should be given to the subordinate;

- Delegate responsibility and authority: don't hang over the person's shoulder watching his/her every move. As long as s/he gets the expected results, let him/her choose how s/he wants to do it;
- Get constant feedback about the project's progress through regular meetings and written reports;
- Maintain good communication lines;
- If the project's progress is slower than expected, do not take the job away from the subordinate; rather work with him/her and encourage him/her to take responsibility for it; and
- Evaluate and reward performance.

Delegation and responsibility

It is important to emphasise that when a manager delegates responsibility and authority to a person to perform certain tasks, s/he still has the responsibility to ensure that the work is of the same standard that it would have been if the manager had been involved. Delegating responsibility and authority to another person does not remove accountability from the manager.

4.4. Task management

The first step in managing a task well is to define the activity clearly. If the task is done by the manager and the employees or volunteers, there can be a strong sense of ownership by all those involved. It is essential to identify the resources and people required to complete the activity. Drawing up a plan is important to ensure the task is achieved.

The objectives, responsibilities and accountability lines should be established by agreement and delegation. This can take place only after the manager has considered the resources and the people and has drawn up a plan to complete the activity. Each activity in a plan comprises a number of tasks. More useful information on drawing up effective plans can be found in the *Project Management* notebook in this series.

The plan must have set standards and reporting boundaries to ensure the task's success.

Example

You need a team to organise a workshop. You need a budget limit. If you do not have a budget limit, team members might plan a workshop that is too expensive and they might waste time because they will have to start from scratch again. Once you have set the budget limit, explain it to team members so they know the bounds within which they are working.

Monitor the performance and progress of everyone in the team. If things are not going according to the plan, the methods and the targets, some aspects might have to be adjusted.

4.5. Managing the group

To manage the group it is necessary to establish, agree on and communicate standards of performance and behaviour. The roles within the group should be identified, developed and agreed on by its members. It is important to develop team work, cooperation, morale and team spirit.

The manager should motivate the group and establish a collective sense of purpose. It is the manager's responsibility to enable, facilitate and ensure effective internal and external group communications. And, if necessary, the manager needs to resolve group conflict, struggles or disagreements.

More details on how to manage groups effectively can be found in the *Project Management* notebook in this series.

4.6. Managing the individual

First it is important to understand that team members are individuals; they have different personalities, skills, strengths, aims, needs and fears. The manager must help and support different individuals in the team.

S/he needs to identify, develop and use each individual's capabilities and strengths and then identify and agree on appropriate individual responsibilities and objectives. Remember to recognise the effort and good work of individuals and, where appropriate, reward individuals with extra responsibilities, advancement and status.

As a manager, your job will be made easier if you can balance the needs of the team, the individuals and the task.

4.7. Communications management

Effective communication is essential in any organisation. Organisations that communicate tend to be more successful. Usually it is the job of managers to ensure successful communication. Like all other management functions it is important to think about communication in a deliberate and conscious way. The following guidelines will help you to ensure strong internal communication:

- All employees should write weekly reports to their supervisors to ensure they and their supervisors understand the tasks at hand and to help plan the processes effectively;
- Hold general monthly meetings to review recent successes and the overall condition of the organisation. The employees should describe their roles to the rest of the members, both staff and volunteers. This will help foster teamwork in your CBO; and
- Hold monthly one-on-one meetings with supervisors to ensure more efficient time management and supervision.

4.8. Time management

Time needs to be managed to guarantee personal effectiveness at work. To manage your time better, you need to:

- Use a form of record-keeping that suits you best. It might be a diary, electronic diary, notebook, a cellphone, etc;
- Categorise your tasks into: routine tasks, ongoing projects, planning and development;
- Analyse your tasks: list them in order – important and urgent, either important or urgent (but not both), neither important nor urgent;
- Prioritise your tasks, plan your time agenda and keep the process moving: time often seems to run out before the task is complete, so time management is important; and
- Be disciplined and committed to self-improvement. The best managers also are the best time managers usually. There are many practical techniques that can help you to become a more effective time

manager. There are several books on time management that you can read to get useful tips.

In CBOs time management is critical because, if is not managed properly, the community might lose faith in your organisation. It can be difficult to ensure effective time management among volunteers. People need to understand the importance of effective time management. This might mean helping people to develop time management skills themselves.

Saying:
'If you steal my time you are committing a crime!'
For many people time is money. If you do not respect their time they might think that you are 'stealing' their money. If you respect other people's time they will respect yours.

Remember that you often need to plan your time. For example, if you need to be at a council meeting at 11am and you have to use public transport, you need to plan to arrive at least half an hour before. Then, if your taxi is late, you will still arrive on time and, if your taxi is early, you can use the time to familiarise yourself with the council agenda.

4.9. Meeting procedures

Meetings can be informal or formal. They are ideal opportunities for individuals to get together to discuss issues of common concern and to make decisions. Meetings are necessary to discuss views and resolve issues.

Managers should plan meetings well, so that they are taken seriously.

Meetings are held for different reasons, such as:

- To give and/or obtain information in order to make decisions;
- To update members on the developments within and outside the organisation; and
- To evaluate the progress of the organisation's work.

If you are planning a meeting, consider the following:

- All staff members and/or volunteers should be informed about the meeting (by word-of-mouth, e-mails, notice board, etc);
- Provide details of the venue and time;
- Ensure that all necessary records and equipment are available at the meeting;
- Distribute the agenda of the meeting on time, so that everyone attending will know what to expect;
- Prepare an attendance register and other relevant documents before the meeting; and
- Evaluate the meeting venue and its conditions.

It is important to keep a record of the meeting in writing: this is called a minute. A minute might include only the decisions taken or it can register everything said by all participants. It will include:

- The date, time and place of the meeting;
- A list of people who attended the meeting and a list of the people who were absent;
- Adoption of previous minutes;
- Discussion on issues from the previous meeting;
- Discussion on new issues;
- Tabling of relevant mailing;
- Decisions taken on operational matters;
- The closure of the meeting; and
- The date, time and place of the next meeting.

Depending on the context and the reason for the meeting, the conduct of the meeting can range from formal to informal. A meeting between contracting parties is likely to be more formal; a meeting between team members might be informal.

For a meeting to be effective there are some key characters, such as:

The chairperson
S/he is responsible for leading and ensuring progress in the meeting.

The secretary
S/he is responsible for preparing the minute and other documents for the meeting.

The treasurer
S/he is responsible for reporting on the financial affairs (income and expenditure) of the organisation.

The members/participants
They will ensure that the meeting has a quorum and they can express their views and pass resolutions.

To sum up, good meetings are held when there is a specific need for them, the outcome of the meeting and the decisions taken are clear and the result is a plan of action. This means that clear targets and deadlines are established and the correct duties and responsibilities are allocated to appropriate staff members.

4.10. Human resources management

Human resources management deals with the recruitment, placement, training and development of staff members or volunteers in an organisation. Human resources management never stops, because change is constant in the working environment and it affects all members of the working community. This process is an ongoing activity that should supply the organisations (including non-governmental groups) with the right people for the right position at the right time.

You might not think that the formal processes that apply to business organisation also apply to CBOs, but internationally it has been shown that often not enough thought is given to the management of volunteers. It is likely that many of the people who carry out the tasks and activities of your CBO will be volunteers. For volunteers to feel satisfied that they are making a contribution, you should apply some of the formal processes of human resource management and adapt them to your CBO environment.

Consider some of the following:

Human resource planning

The planning process is affected by internal and external factors. Internal factors include skills needs, vacancies, departmental expansions and/or reductions. External factors include salary levels, the labour market, technology, etc.

Recruitment

Refers to locating candidates for a specific job vacancy or volunteer position. This can be done through word of mouth, advertising in newspapers, engaging employment agencies, using bulletin boards and circulating vacancy notices, etc.

Selection

You can use standardised measures (such as application forms, résumés, interviews, skills tests and reference checks etc) to assess and evaluate the candidates and to select the best one for the job.

Socialisation/induction

It is important to consider how the selected candidate will fit into the organisation. You need to familiarise the selected candidate with the work processes, procedures, co-workers and the organisation's mission, policies and culture etc.

Training and development

It is important that the organisation adopt training and education policies to ensure lifelong education and training of personnel and volunteers. This will guarantee that workers are able to contribute to the organisation's objectives.

Performance appraisal

This will ensure an ongoing assessment of the individual and how the person fits into an organisation and helps to achieve its mission.

Promotions, transfers, dismissals

An individual's value to the organisation needs to be assessed. High performers might be transferred to other sections or promoted and low performers might have to be dismissed after the necessary warnings.

It is important to remember that if your organisation has paid employees that *CBOs are subject to the country's labour legislation.* CBOs must provide written contracts of employment for each employee. These should indicate clearly the conditions of employment, including job description and salary. The benefits and obligations of staff should be included in the conditions of employment, which should be available to all employees before the contract is signed. CBOs also have to comply with government regulations regarding payment for taxes and other levies on behalf of their employees.

Ongoing human resource planning, selection, training and appraisal will guarantee the success of an organisation.

4.11. Conflict management

Conflict can occur between individuals or groups of people; it is the expression of differences between them and it can be peaceful or violent. Generally conflict is about power and interests. One person or group might want more power than another.

Conflict management is useful, because it can prevent the conflict from getting worse, improves cooperation between the group members, motivates the group and builds trust and consensus.

Conflict can be managed in different ways:

Negotiation

Is used when individuals or parties involved in the conflict agree to seek to reach an agreement by adjusting their views and positions in a joint effort to achieve consensus, while still preserving their interests as much as possible.

Joint problem-solving

The parties involved seek to reach an agreement by identifying the causes of it, generating alternative solutions and jointly agreeing on viable solutions to the conflict.

Facilitation

Is a voluntary process in which a third party (not involved in the conflict) manages a discussion between the parties.

Mediation

Is also a voluntary process in which a third party helps the disputing parties to arrive at an agreed solution. The process of mediation is a more formal process. It is likely that mediation will be used only when other methods have failed.

The role of the mediator is:

- To stop the argument;
- To give each party involved in the conflict the chance to give his/her side without the interference of the other party;
- To ask the parties involved for possible solutions;
- To choose the best solution; and
- Get agreement on solution.

Arbitration

Is a formalised legal process. Two parties will present their cases to a third party – usually a lawyer or a judge or, if internal, to a panel of people appointed by the organisation. Once the positions of the two parties have been heard, a decision will be made on their behalf. This decision is binding and cannot be renegotiated.

5. Management in context

You might find that even though you apply all the skills consistently there is something that is not going right. It might not be something you can lay your finger on exactly, but you know it has something to do with people who approach things differently. Often this different approach can be explained by understanding their cultural contexts. New management thinking helps us to understand that management tools are not neutral and might be affected by culture or the different world views of people working within organisations.

One theory is that there are two different world views present in people in organisations, each of which will have an impact on behaviour in an organisation. One world view is called the high context world view. Often this is seen in operation in countries or cultures that are less industrialised than others. The low context world view is operational in highly industrialised societies. The table below illustrates how being high or low context will affect the people who work in organisations differently.

Value	High Context	Low Context
Time	Cyclical	Linear
Leadership	Skills	Roles
Decision-making	Consensus	Consultation
Task & Maintenance	Relational	Rational
Communication	Oral	Written
Concept of self	Community Organisation Individual	Individual Organisation Community
World view	Spiritual	Scientific

The different ways people work together are not better or worse, just different. You might find that in some circumstances you will need people who are more high-context oriented, while in others you will need people who are more low-context oriented. You will find that almost all people have a combination of the two contexts. As a manager, it would be useful to identify which world view is in operation. This could help to minimise frustration when managing people and processes.

6. Conclusion

This notebook has covered the basics of CBO management. It should be used as a guide to the daily management tasks of a CBO. If the concepts are used regularly they will become routine in time.

A CBO is a non-profit organisation that provides social services at the local level. Although management can be interpreted differently, most people acknowledge that it is a process of different activities: planning; organising; leading and coordinating. All these activities are equally important and should be carefully studied.

For management in CBOs to be effective it is important for the manager to be well prepared and aware of her/his functions. The main task of a manager is to coordinate all the different activities of the management process successfully.

Management is a difficult skill and might take years to master. It is never easy and can also be quite lonely sometimes. You might not be popular if you are a good manager, but you will ensure that your organisation meets its goals.

It is important in Africa that we have a vibrant, well-functioning civil society. CBOs have an important role to play when it comes to strengthening democracy. Effective management will ensure stronger CBOs and, therefore, stronger democracies.

7. References

Books

Camay, P. & Gordon, A. J. *Principles of NGO Management.* CORE, Johannesburg, 1997.

Edwards, M. & Fowler, A. (eds.) *The earthscan reader on NGO Management.* Earthscan Publications Ltd, London, 2002.

Manuals

2005. IDASA. *Basics of CBO Management.*

2004. IDASA. *Community Based Organisations (CBOs) Management.*

Websites

Rural Livelihoods Evaluation Partnership
http://www.livelihoods.org/lessons/Asia/RLEP_CBM_Summary.pdf#search='Community Based Organisation Management'
[Accessed on September 14, 2005]

Center for Health Care Strategies
http://www.chcs.org/info-url3968/info-url.htm
[Accessed on September 14, 2005]

IDASA
http://www.idasa.org.za
[Accessed on September 14, 2005]

AIDSinfo
http://aidsinfo.nih.gov/ed_resources/glossary/default.asp?id=174&letter=c
[Accessed on September 14, 2005]

Free, On-Line Nonprofit Organisation and Management Development Program
http://www.managementhelp.org/np_progs/org_dev.htm
[Accessed on September 14, 2005]

PROJECT MANAGEMENT

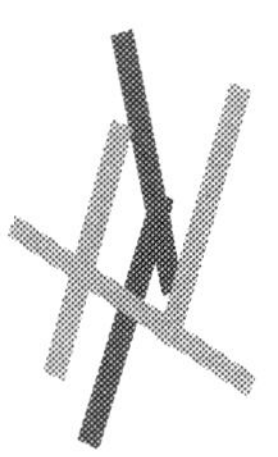

1. Introduction

There are increasing opportunities for community-based organisations (CBOs) to sustain themselves. They can do this by accessing funding or by tendering through local government structures. However, CBOs are expected to be able to manage the finances and the deliverables in a professional manner, which also ensures that projects are successfully implemented.

To achieve this most effectively it is necessary to improve the management of projects. CBOs are not new to managing projects, but usually the approach is instinctive, driven by discussion, trial and error. This can lead to frustration for the parties involved. The principles of project management might be familiar to CBOs because many are practising some of these principles on a daily basis already, but it is useful to have a disciplined framework, with tools and techniques to enhance the existing capacity in CBOs. It also helps CBOs if there is always sufficient documentation of these processes.

It has been shown in the private and government sectors that project management is a useful formal tool for organisations to run their projects more successfully. If CBOs are able to implement this approach it can improve development at a local level. This will benefit the communities that need service delivery the most.

This notebook is by no means a comprehensive guide to project management, but should rather be seen as an introduction to the principles and an easy-to-use resource. The notebook tries to put project management principles into a language that CBOs can use. Once you feel comfortable working with the guide, you should feel free to develop your knowledge through further reading and study.

2. Understanding the concept of project management

There are many definitions of project management. In all these definitions there are some key common points. Project management aims to:

- Achieve certain outcomes within a specific time period;
- Use good planning;
- Schedule tasks properly; and
- Make the most of available resources, including money, materials, equipment and people.

Project management is a formal process. It uses tools to ensure that:

- Detailed tasks are identified and laid out;
- Responsible people are allocated to the tasks;
- Measurable objectives are put in place to ensure that targets are met;
- Changes are made in time to ensure targets can be met;
- The budget is well controlled;
- The correct allocation of equipment and materials is made throughout the lifespan of the project.

The process of project management usually allocates responsibility to one person – known as the project manager – to monitor the progress of a team of people working together to achieve the overall outcome of the project.

Example

A group of young South Africans is organising a Youth Day celebration. This might include activities such as sport, arts and culture and a political memorial event. To achieve success on 16 June they will need to start working months ahead of time. They must have an effective plan that mobilises resources (money, people, equipment etc). The plan should be used constantly as a working document. Using the plan will enable the team members to determine if they are on track to achieve all their outcomes. They can allocate responsibilities to different members of the team. They can use the project plan document to measure their progress. It can also be used to make their team meetings effective and task-focused. They might find that even though they planned to have two people working on sports, two people working on arts and culture and two people working on the political memorial activity, it turns out that organising sports is easy. They should then consider having only one person working on sports and maybe three people working on the arts and culture activity. They also might have to redirect money and equipment to arts and culture.

When the project objectives are achieved it is necessary to ensure the project is completed often. This is an aspect of project management that is often neglected, because people are more excited about starting and achieving their goals. However, it is necessary to ensure reports are written up and all materials are returned if necessary. The team must be debriefed. Lessons must be written up or documented for future activities.

3. Overview of the project management elements

This section will show you the elements that make up project management. We will deal with most of these areas in more detail. Project management is broken down into the following elements:

1. **Project scope management**
   This refers to the planning of the project. You must think about all the elements that will make up your project in detail before you begin planning.

2. **Project time management**
   This is an important aspect of project management. You need to make sure that you plan in detail how much time an activity will take and ensure that your goals are realistic and achievable. During the project you might have to make adjustments if you are not meeting the targets you have set.

3. **Project cost management**
   This is also a key element of project management. It is important to manage a project within its budget. Underspending can be as dangerous as overspending. Good planning and paying close attention to spending money carefully will mean that you can achieve all the goals you set for your project.

4. **Project quality management**
   This aspect is more relevant in fields like construction, where the builders have to make sure that all technical specifications are met to a high standard. But it is important when delivering projects in the community that you do so to the best of your ability.

5. **Project human resource management**
   You need to make sure that you identify the skills you will need for the project. Make sure you use the skills of the people working on the project in the most effective way possible. Project teams also need to work together effectively. There are tools to help you to do this. There are also ways of thinking about people and the day-to-day dynamics that will affect your project. These tools are included later in the notebook.

6. **Project communication management**
   It is useful to plan how you will communicate with stakeholders, donors and the project team. This will ensure that the project is implemented in a smooth manner.

7. **Project risk management**
   There is always the possibility that things might go wrong during a project. It helps to think at the beginning of a project about what these risks might be. If you have considered all the risks involved, you will be in a better position to manage the changes you might need to make during the implementation of the project.

8. **Project procurement management**
   This sounds fancy, but it refers to how you manage the buying of goods and services during the project.

9. **Project integration management**
   You will see later in the notebook that there are many different elements that you must think about when implementing a project. This aspect of project management will help to ensure that you are always in

control of all the different activities taking place. This means the project manager must be aware of all the different elements and how they fit together during the course of a project.

We will examine each of these principles in relation to CBOs and unpack the 'jargon' used to make the concept of project management more user-friendly.

4. Project context

A key element to successful project management is thinking about the context in which the project must work. When we refer to context we are talking about the 'internal' environment and the 'external' environment.

The internal environment refers to the organisation itself:

- Will the project be out of place in the organisation?
- Will it drain resources from other projects?
- Does the rest of the organisation agree that the project is a good idea?

The external environment refers to the community in which the project will be delivered and the broader political environment. For example, ten years ago people who encouraged the youth to wear condoms during sex encountered a hostile environment. But this has changed somewhat because of more awareness of HIV/AIDS.

A hostile internal or external environment can lead to a project not achieving its goals. So, before embarking on a planning exercise, it is useful to do an analysis to inform you of what factors need to be considered. It will also result in a project that is well thought out.

It is within this context that the project life cycle takes place. Each stage of the project life cycle is a broad theme under which the different elements of project management will play themselves out on a practical level.

5. The project life cycle

The project life cycle is made up of the following four key areas:

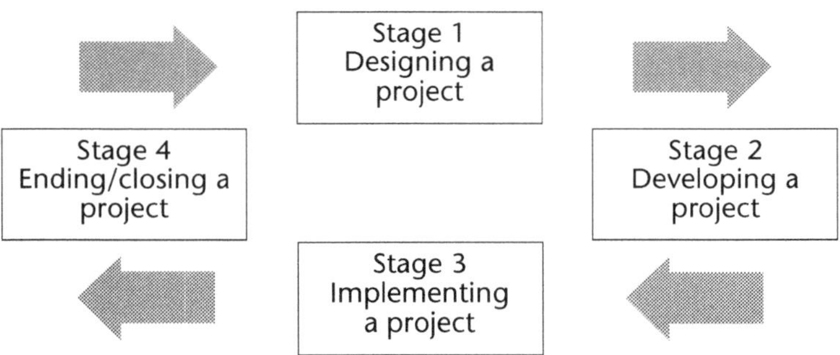

It is the project life cycle that is critical to successful project management. Between each stage evaluations should take place. Agreements must be made on how to improve the next steps of the project. The evaluation might change the sequence in which the next steps will take place.

To ensure the smooth running of each stage the following list is a guide for activities that *MUST* take place at each stage for the life cycle to proceed smoothly. You will notice that some of the elements are specific steps that should take place during each stage.

5.1. Designing of project

- Collect as much information as possible;
- Identify what kind of need your project will address in your community;
- Establish goals and objectives for your project;
- Draw up a financial plan or budget;

- Think about what risks your project might face and possible solutions;
- Think about who your team members could be;
- Identify alternative options;
- Write up your proposal;
- Present your proposal; and
- Obtain approval for the next phase.

5.2. Developing the project

- Appoint team members;
- Conduct research if needed;
- Develop your project plan;
- Present your project plan to all stakeholders; and
- Obtain approval to proceed.

5.3. Implementation

- Organise all the tasks;
- Communicate with all the people who need to know what is being achieved during the project;
- Motivate the team;
- Make sure that everyone knows what each person must do, that the team members know the deadlines and establish a means for you, as project manager, to ensure that they have completed their activities successfully;
- Be clear about how you will write up all the achievements;
- Buy goods and services;
- Monitor the overall goals and objectives of the project by making sure that the service is of a high standard, is delivered on time and that all costs are kept as low as possible; and
- Resolve problems.

5.4. Ending/closing

- Complete all outstanding activities;
- Write reports;
- Evaluate the project and ensure that the donors or funders are satisfied;
- Release or redirect resources; and
- Reassign the project team.

You now have a broad overview of the basic steps that make up project management. Now you need to examine each element in detail. It is important that, as you read through these elements, you constantly try to remember which stage of the project life cycle they belong to. In some cases there might be an overlap between an element and a stage.

Keep in mind where the overlaps might be or you could miss some steps in the project management plan because you believe you have already completed a stage in the project life cycle.

6. A detailed look at the elements

6.1. Project scope management

This is the beginning of the project and the most critical aspect of the project management process. To ensure that all the above categories are covered, the project manager will need to ensure that a project proposal is prepared. There are various tools that can be used to prepare a project proposal, but one of the most commonly used tools is the *logical framework analysis* (LFA).

The LFA requires detailed and disciplined thinking to cover all the aspects that make up a project. This includes:

- Why it should be done;
- What are the possibilities for mistakes; and

- What checking mechanisms are in place to ensure that achievements within the project plan can be measured.

The first step in the LFA is to conduct a background analysis to establish:

- Why the problem exists;
- What led to the problem;
- Why it is necessary to have a project to address the problem;
- Who will benefit from the project;
- Why another project might not be more successful than this project;
- Why your organisation should be the one to tackle the project;
- Who the stakeholders are; and
- What the project might achieve.

You should write this up as the introduction to the proposal or plan.

This analysis needs to be done before you write the project proposal. It is usually called the background to the project.

Once you have written up the background, you need to begin planning your project. Draw up a table to ensure your thinking and planning is disciplined and detailed. The following table is an example of how to structure your thinking and planning:

Objectives	Performance indicators	Means of verification
Developmental goal (What is the long-term impact of your project on the developmental problem?)	Measurable Indicators for long-term goal	Information sources
For example: The goal of the project will be to make sure that all people in the community know how to manage HIV/AIDS effectively and compassionately	For example: People living with HIV/ AIDS are treated with respect by their family and other community members People living with HIV/ AIDS feel loved and supported by their family, the medical staff at their clinic or hospital and the broader community	For example: Interviews with ten people living with HIV/ AIDS at the beginning of the project and then again at the end of the project
Project Purpose (What is the immediate impact, ie what will the project achieve?)	Measurable indicators for end of project impact	Information sources
For example: The project will educate and inform family members about HIV/ AIDS in general; the medical treatment of HIV/AIDS; what human care and love can achieve for people living with HIV/AIDS	For example: Four public awareness events; four workshops with family members	For example: Posters and pamphlets; photographs; registration forms; evaluation forms; flipcharts and workshop reports
Project Outputs (The actual products or deliverables of the project)	Measurable indicators for outputs	Information sources
For example: Research with people living with HIV/AIDS; a play about living with HIV/AIDS; ten community ambassadors who are family members, medical staff and local government councillors	For example: Research report; actors, script and venues with a stage; ten committed people who continue to give talks and inspire the community	For example: Questionnaires; interviews; photographs; video of the play; a pledge of commitment signed by each ambassador

(continued on page 12)

Objectives	Performance	Means of verification
Project Activities	Inputs, people, materials and equipment	Information sources
For example: The play – hold a mini-workshop to ask people living with HIV/AIDS what they think should be in play; write a script; recruit volunteer actors; rehearse the play; make costumes; make the set; have a dress rehearsal; stage the play on a public awareness day	For example: Director; script writer; actors; costume makers; make-up people; pamphlets; posters; loudhailer to recruit people to come to the event; material for costumes; make-up; photocopied scripts for all the actors; a venue to practise; invitations for friends to come to the dress rehearsal	For example: Photographs; video; actor register for rehearsals; receipts for material; receipts for make-up; document that shows agreement with community centre for rehearsal space; attendance at play

The rest of the project proposal should cover the following aspects:

- Budget;
- Work plan or Gantt chart (which can include the critical path method);
- Outline of the project manager's responsibilities (job description); and
- The organisational structures which will ensure effective oversight of the project (this refers to the board, the director, the financial manager, etc).

Project scope management therefore means taking note of all the processes of the work required. It should include only the work (or tasks) required to complete the project successfully. The outcomes of this element will be the project plan. All the team members will use this plan to complete the project.

Example

If you and your team members are expected to attend a strategic planning event for your organisation, do not include that in the project scope management because it is not critical to the achievement of the project goals.

You should give yourself a month or two to write the project document. This will give you time to show it to others to get their input in case you missed some details. This is not always possible and you might have to write up the document in a week or less.

6.2. Project time management

To manage your time most effectively there are three tools commonly used in project management to help with good time management. These are:

- The work plan, known as the work breakdown structure (WBS);
- The calendar known as a Gantt chart; and
- The critical path method (CPM).

Each of these tools is used in combination with the others for the best time management during the life of the project.

6.2.1. The WBS

Although this sounds like an intimidating term it really means that you, as a project manager, should think about ALL the activities that will take place during the course of your project and write them up into a work plan.

To begin the work plan or WBS it is important to note what the *main phases* (level one) of your project are, for example, preparation, setting up, implementation, evaluation and termination.

Now under each of these phases you will need to identify all the *main tasks or activities* (level two) that need to take place to ensure the phase is completed.

Example

Setting up activities

- Recruitment of team members;
- Induction of team members to the organisation and to the project proposal and plan;
- Team-building activities;
- Networking; and
- Identifying suppliers, etc.

Then you must go to the next level (level three) and break down each of the main activities into a set of *sub-activities* that will enable you to achieve the overall project goal.

Example

Sub-activities:

Recruitment of team members to achieve the project goal

- Write up job descriptions;
- Circulate positions among existing staff or volunteers in the organisation;
- Advertise position in community and regional newspapers;
- Seek help from a recruitment agency if necessary;
- Set a deadline for CV submissions;
- Collect all CVs;
- Shortlist about five potential candidates for each position available;
- Set up interviews;

- Draw up interview questions;
- Select an interview panel;
- Design or use an existing human resource tool to evaluate candidates;
- Conduct interviews;
- Make a decision as a panel;
- Contact successful candidate to arrange the first working day and induction process;
- Set up a work station for new team member; and
- Contact unsuccessful candidates with a thank you letter.

This example was compiled using what is known as the *top-down approach.*

An alternative would be to list all the detailed activities that need to take place to make the project a success. Then you can group them into phases. Now you can decide the order in which each phase should take place. This is known as the *bottom-up approach.*

Once you have all the detailed activities you can begin to arrange them into the formal tool known as the WBS. The WBS will help you, as the project manager or as a team member, to identify which tasks should take place before other tasks. For example, you would not be able to conduct interviews if you had not had tasks to help you identify candidates for the positions in the team.

It is important to identify:

- How long each task will take;
- How many people are required for each task to be completed; and
- What function they will serve on the project, for example, book-keeper, engineer, community facilitator, etc.

6.2.1.1. What is the WBS?

The work breakdown structure or WBS is the key baseline tool which will help to ensure that the rest of the tools are effective. The more detail that is included in compiling this tool the better you will be able to use the other tools in combination with the WBS. The WBS diagram (see page 19) will show clearly all the activities that must take place for the project to be successful.

6.2.1.2. Why is a WBS necessary?

- It helps to divide the project into small work packages, tasks or activities;
- It helps project managers to identify the required tasks;
- It helps to obtain consensus on the work to be done; and
- It helps to make sure the tasks or activities match the timeframes or schedule and cost estimates.

6.2.1.3. How do you compile a WBS?

Once you have a list of all the activities, you should put them into a diagram. This diagram is known as the WBS.

The following diagram is an example of what a WBS will look like:

FOOD SECURITY PROJECT

Selection of project area	Workshop 1	Research/ info. gathering	Facilitation of access to land	Workshop 2	Capacity building
List criteria for several beneficiaries	Identify and integrate reps into PSC	Baseline study of beneficiaries	Scan govt and non-profit organisation (NPO) programmes	Workshop options to beneficiaries	Dev materials for capacity building
Integrate with CSO	Present projects to beneficiaries	Baseline study of land rights	Identify land needs	PSC facilitates interaction between programme and service providers	Organise training for beneficiary groups
Identify and meet potential groups	Wks proceedings	Submit research report to PSC	Identify support orgs. govt. and NPOs	Workshop evaluation	
Form project steering comm. (PSC)	Prepare wks proceedings	Beneficiaries group selects option			

The above diagram is a WBS for a CBO project based in Ghana – many similar projects are in operation throughout Africa. Some receive funds from international donors. Others are funded through the social welfare programmes of provincial, regional or local government agencies (Frimpong 2003:59).

The WBS will help you to compile a calendar or Gantt chart and a realistic budget.

When you compile your WBS it is useful to identify the *start and end dates* for each activity. By doing this you will be able to identify the activities that overlap.

If you know which activities overlap you will be able to see which activities can put you ahead of schedule. When project managers talk about *lead time* they are referring to being ahead of time.

Some overlapping activities might cause a delay and can put you behind schedule and are referred to as *lag time* activities.

The WBS will enable you to identify the critical points of the project. These are important because they could lead to failure if one activity overruns an end date by too much time.

In other words, you are trying to identify which activities need to happen by a certain time so that they do not delay the rest of the project.

Once you have completed these steps it is important to give the project plan to all relevant stakeholders or parties. You should get approval, comments, additions or changes. This will save you a lot of time further down the line. You might have to motivate people to give in their comments by the time you need them. Now you can use the information to create a calendar, also known as a Gantt chart.

6.2.2. The calendar or Gantt chart

All work plans need to have a calendar to make sure they are completed on time. In project management this is a bar chart, known as a Gantt chart because a man called Henry Gantt invented this tool in the early 1900s.

It is used to schedule all the activities before the start of the project. A bar chart is a tool that lays out all the tasks horizontally, allowing all members or stakeholders to get an overall view of the time frames expected for the project to be completed.

It is important to emphasise that the Gantt chart must include all the activities from the WBS to be most effective.

You should first develop a Gantt chart for the main activities. Then you must develop a chart that includes the sub-activities so that all team members understand the deadlines for their activities.

Bar charts are a commonly used tool in project management. One of its many advantages is its simplicity. You can either draw it by hand or you can design one using a computer – if you have funds you can buy project management software.

The following diagram (see page 22) is an example of a bar or Gantt chart using the WBS shown in the previous diagram.

The next Gantt chart (see page 23) highlights the level three sub-activities and the level two main activities.

The black blocks refer to the amount of time the whole activity will take and the light gray blocks refer to the time each sub-activity will take.

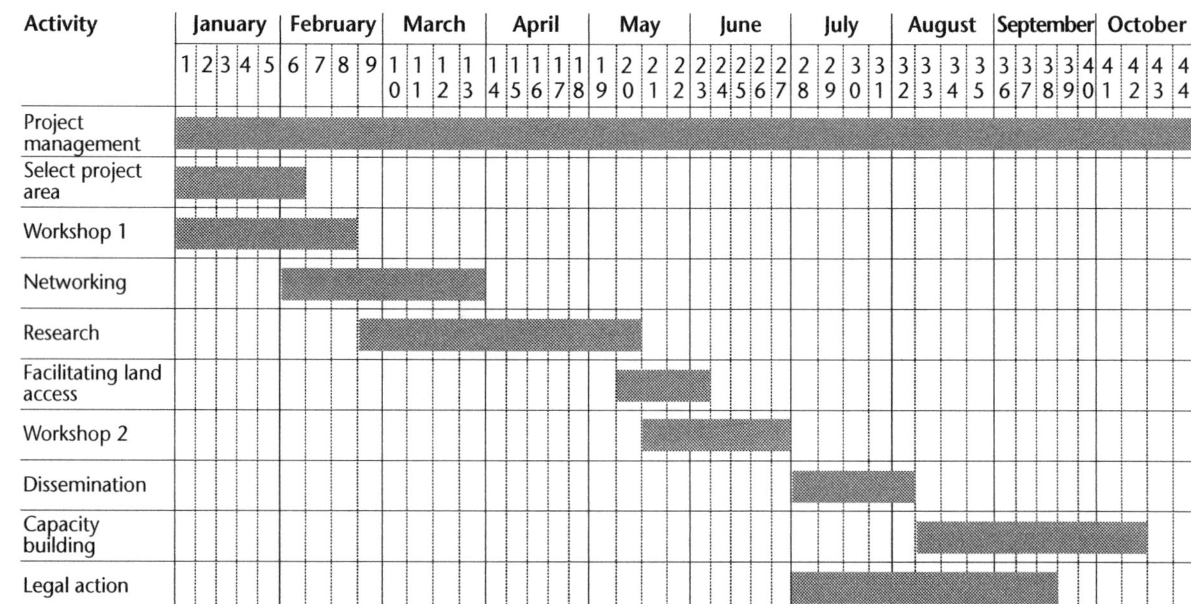

Please note that in the above diagram the start and end dates refer to early finish and early start dates

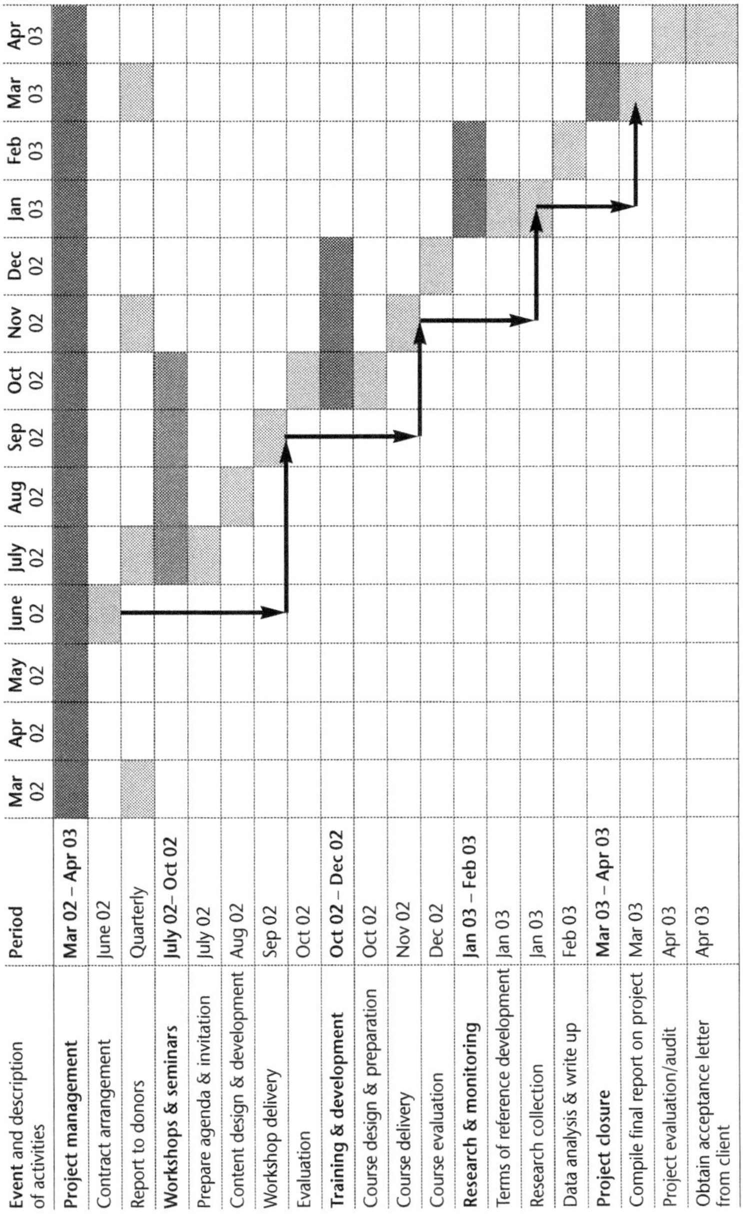

Event and description of activities	Period	Mar 02	Apr 02	May 02	June 02	July 02	Aug 02	Sep 02	Oct 02	Nov 02	Dec 02	Jan 03	Feb 03	Mar 03	Apr 03
Project management	**Mar 02 – Apr 03**														
Contract arrangement	June 02														
Report to donors	Quarterly														
Workshops & seminars	**July 02– Oct 02**														
Prepare agenda & invitation	July 02														
Content design & development	Aug 02														
Workshop delivery	Sep 02														
Evaluation	Oct 02														
Training & development	**Oct 02 – Dec 02**														
Course design & preparation	Oct 02														
Course delivery	Nov 02														
Course evaluation	Dec 02														
Research & monitoring	**Jan 03 – Feb 03**														
Terms of reference development	Jan 03														
Research collection	Jan 03														
Data analysis & write up	Feb 03														
Project closure	**Mar 03 – Apr 03**														
Compile final report on project	Mar 03														
Project evaluation/audit	Apr 03														
Obtain acceptance letter from client	Apr 03														

6.2.3. The CPM

The critical path method or CPM is used to determine the length of a project and to identify the activities that are critical to complete a project.

The following steps should be followed to draw a CPM diagram:

- Specify the individual activities;
- Determine the flow of activities, for example, what activity should follow another;
- Estimate the completion time for each activity; and
- Identify the critical path of the project.

The critical path refers to which activities must take place before another activity can take place.

Example

You cannot write the project report in the beginning – it has to take place at the end of the project.

Using the Gantt chart you will be able to identify the total time it will take for the project to run.

You should also update your chart during the project so that you can see what project activities are taking longer (or shorter) than expected.

If an activity that does *not* depend on other activities takes longer it will not matter. But if one of the activities that is *critical* to a number of other activities takes longer, you will encounter problems and might have to negotiate for a longer time period to deliver the project.

You can draw the critical path on to the Gantt chart – in our example of a Gantt chart the bold arrows are drawn from each critical activity to the next to show the critical path.

6.3. Project cost management

If you have used the LFA tool and have a detailed WBS, you will have paid a great deal of attention to planning resources already. These two tools give you a good idea of how much money you will need to raise. To plan effectively for your budget you will need to look at all the activities you have listed and estimate how much the project will cost.

6.3.1. Drawing up the budget

It is important to think in as much detail as possible when you are drawing up a budget. As far as is possible, try to draw up the budget based on real costs. If your budget is for a two-year project, factor in inflation. Although many CBOs might not have staff costs, you must remember that volunteers cost money because they use resources, such as telephones and faxes, and there are transport costs and food costs etc.

This was the budget for the Food Security Project in Ghana:

Line item	Amount
Programme costs	
Salaries (programme staff)	56 000
Benefits (programme staff)	1 400
Accommodation/venue for workshop	4 000
Facilitators	900
Travel/field trip expenses	32 000
Per diem	9 000
Printing and stationery	800
Consultants fees	8 000
Advertising	5 000
Vehicle	600
Vehicle expenses	1 800
Resource development/training	600
Research	4 000
Equipment	8 000
Total	**136 600**

Please note that although the size of the budget is quite large in the example, this will not be the case for most CBOs. It is important to be aware of the line items because they should be considered when drawing up budgets.

Example

You might not have vehicles in your budget, but you might need to budget for the use of public transport.

It is important to note that different funders and different government departments will have different rules for what they will finance and what they will not finance. You should not submit the general budget for each request for funding, but should adapt the budget according to the funder's guidelines.

Other key areas *the project manager must keep effective financial control of are:*

- Travel/expense vouchers/receipts;
- Invoices;
- Cheque requisitions;
- Payments;
- Time sheets for team members and consultants;
- Monthly financial statements;
- Financial reporting by the project manager to the director or board;
- Asset register;
- Annual financial report; and
- Audit.

6.4. Project quality management

It is important for a project manager and the team members to take the quality of delivery of a project as seriously as a multinational corporation does. The better CBOs become at quality management at a local level the more likely communities are to benefit from decentralised service delivery that is sensitive to the needs of the community. CBOs are often the closest organisations to the community and understand the needs of the community. Your CBO should always strive to be as professional as possible.

Example *Running a workshop*

Facilitators should hold a planning meeting to establish who should do what during the course of the day;
Facilitators should have ALL their materials; and
Facilitators should be there before the workshop is scheduled to begin.

The most challenging aspect for CBOs is to focus as much attention on the technical aspects of project management as they do on stakeholder consultations.

6.5. Project human resource management

As is the case in all businesses, government agencies and NPOs, the people are *always* the most valuable resource in ensuring effective delivery. The *team members* need to be *carefully selected, trained and effectively supported* throughout the lifespan of the project. You must give team members constant encouragement and recognition for their work.

Leadership is crucial in project management. Generally, project managers have to exercise considerable leadership skills.

Management can be defined as the art of getting others to do what you cannot necessarily do yourself, by organising, controlling and directing resources.

Leadership is the ability to identify what has to be done and then to select the people who are best able to tackle it. Leadership is also about setting goals and objectives and generating enthusiasm. Choosing the right project leader is critical to the success of any project.

The characteristics of a good project manager
who will be the leader of the project team are:

- Positive attitude;
- Common sense;
- Open-mindedness;
- Adaptability;
- Inventiveness;
- Prudent risk-taker;
- Fairness; and
- Commitment.

Effective teamwork is important in good project management. All groups can be expected to go through five stages. They might move back and forth between two stages before they move on to the next one. It is up to the project manager to help the group to move on to the next stage to achieve the goals of the project.

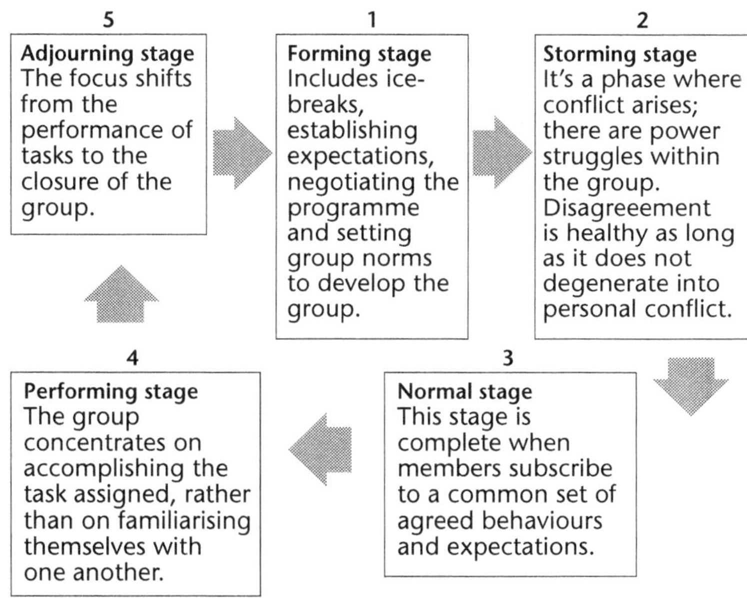

Conflict can occur at all levels in projects. This is largely because there might be many different parties working together with their own aims. At some point the parties might clash or their aims will have changed. Projects and contracts can create conflict. Motivation will be required among the project team and stakeholders to resolve conflict.

Resolution of conflicts between individual members of the team are important elements of teamwork. The diversity of the team members should be considered because this can also lead to conflict.

Conflict management is the art of managing and resolving conflict creatively and productively. The art of conflict management is to channel these conflicts so that the result is positive rather than destructive.

6.6. Project Communication Management

Good communication with all stakeholders will help to ensure your project is a success. A communication plan is often developed at the start of a project.

The methods of communication can include:

- Verbal communication;
- Body language can convey messages;
- Written communication on paper; and
- Electronic communication such as email, etc.

The content and the manner of delivery are perhaps more important than the method used.

Formal meetings are an important aspect of communication but can, if not managed correctly, result in a waste of time, money and energy.

Certain meetings play a structural or process role in projects, for example, the inaugural meeting which is required at a project launch. Other meetings include design reviews, periodic progress reviews, etc. The project manager should know:

- What meetings are required;
- When they should take place; and
- How they should be conducted.

Information or document management is important for effective communication. This is important not only during the project for documenting decision-making and progress, but also for monitoring and evaluation purposes. Project documents can also be useful when planning future projects.

6.7. Project risk management

Risks are present in all projects, whatever their size or complexity and in whatever industry or business sector. Risks are those factors that might cause a project to fail to meet its objectives.

Once identified and assessed, risks need to be managed so that they do not have a big impact on a project.

Some helpful questions to ask yourself are:

- What will help to achieve the long-term goal of the project?
- What could prevent me from achieving the long-term goal?
- What factors will help the project to achieve success?
- What factors could inhibit the project from achieving success?
- What will help to achieve the outputs?
- What could prevent me and my team from achieving our outputs?
- What will definitely work in relation to the activities?
- Why?

If some of the risks that you identified do occur, you will need to manage the impact of these risks on your project.

Example

You have assumed that you can ask an NGO to help you with the research aspect of your project. Suddenly it can no longer help you because the person that it assigned to work with you has resigned. You should either ask another NGO to help or you will have to do the research on your own without assistance – this might, of course, take longer.

6.8. Project procurement management

Buying new services or products for a project can be costly. If this is not managed well, you will be forced to spend more money on new services and products and less money on workshops or materials.

To make sure you get the best value for money you must ask at least three different suppliers for quotes. Use the cheapest supplier.

If the purchasing process is managed well, substantial savings can be made. These can then be spent on other important processes, such as consultation and skills transfer.

If a project is not managed properly then costs can spiral out of control. Project activities will suffer as a result of a lack of resources.

6.9. Project integration management

Project integration management ensures that *all* the various processes of the project are properly co-ordinated. This is the task of the project manager.

You should always know if all activities, documentation, meetings, financial and control systems are operational and effective. To ensure that your co-ordination is effective you need to pay particular attention to project monitoring and evaluation *throughout* the course of the project. You must not leave it until the end, as often happens.

6.9.1. Project monitoring

The project manager needs to be constantly aware of what is going on in the project. You should check that each activity is taking place and that everyone is doing what they are supposed to be doing. This is called monitoring.

To monitor a project effectively you need to:
- Track progress in terms of the plan;
- Compare actual outcomes with predicted outcomes;
- Check the outputs;
- Collect, record and report information to all the relevant stakeholders and parties;
- Check the impact of the project regularly;
- Check the indicators regularly;
- Take regular photographs of project activities;
- Regularly summarise the results of the indicators; and
- Hold regular meetings to review the monitoring information.

6.9.2. Project evaluation

Evaluation is assessing whether the project goals were achieved in the best way possible and if there was room for improvement in the way the work was done.

To ensure effective evaluation you need to consider:
- The quality and effectiveness of the project;
- The efficiency and effectiveness of the project;
- The budget control; and
- Formative evaluation (this means conducting a baseline study before you begin your project).

There are many tools and techniques that can help you to monitor and evaluate the project. As project manager you might consider attending training courses on these because they can be quite technical, but evaluation is a valuable skill that will stand you and your organisation in good stead.

7. Project ending/closing

The hardest part for the project manager is to ensure that the project is wrapped up properly. The excitement of the activities has ended and all the loose ends must be tied up before a new project can begin. The project manager must ensure that *all* the project objectives or tender requirements have been met. He or she must ensure that all payments have been made. If the project was a tender he or she needs to get a letter of acceptance from the client (for example, the government agency).

The project manager should conduct a post-project evaluation:

- Compare the planned Gantt chart with the actual Gantt chart to establish how accurate the planning tool was;
- Compare the difference between the resources allocated and the actual resources used to establish how realistic planning was;
- Compare the difference between budgeted costs and the real costs – did the project overspend or underspend and was this acceptable. Why did it happen?
- What mistakes were made? What was done to fix them? What should be done differently in the future?
- What went better than expected? Why? Can this happen again?
- Evaluate the management and control functions – this requires an honest assessment. The project manager can draw on others to help with this.
- What new methods were used, what worked and what did not work? What should be used in the future?
- Conduct staff or volunteer evaluations.

8. Conclusion

We have covered all the basic aspects of project management. In this notebook you have been exposed to the theory of project management, but have also seen examples of it.

We hope that CBOs begin to implement the tools and techniques and practise them. They can be effective only if used on a regular basis. Eventually the use of these tools and techniques will become second nature.

We hope that your service delivery is improved through the effective use of project management tools and techniques and that access to more resources becomes a reality for many CBOs.

Resources

Books

1. Frimpong, M., 2003. *Project Management for Non-Profit Organizations: A Practical Guide for Managing Developmental Projects.* Repro Centre. Johannesburg.

Manuals

1. Commission of the European Communities, 1993. *Project Cycle Management: Integrated Approach and Logical Framework. No 1.* February. Ceuterick. Leuven.
2. Olive, 1998. *Project Planning for Development: The Project Planning Handbook,* July. Olive Publications.

Websites

1. 02 July 2005.
   www.apm.org.uk
2. 03 July 2005.
   www.buildersnet.org/cpmtutor/cpmtutorial
3. 05 July 2005.
   www.NetMBA.com/operations/project/cpm
4. 05 July 2005.
   www.ifors.ms.unimelb.edu.au/cpmtutorial/about/cpm.about.html
5. 06 July 2005.
   www.1stManager.com

ADVOCACY AND COMMUNICATION

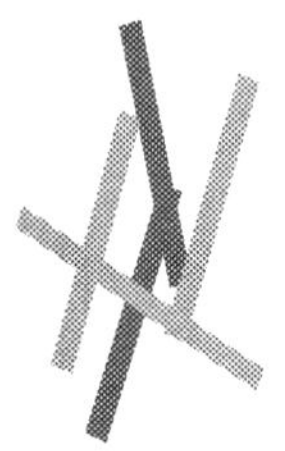

1. Introduction

In a democratic society there are many different groups which might have competing interests. You need to make your voice heard and get your viewpoint across to achieve your vision. The formal terminology for this process is **advocacy, lobbying** and **communication**.

To do this most effectively, tools are available to community-based organisations (CBOs). Advocacy, lobbying and communication are the key approaches to ensure the community in which you work is best served by your CBO.

Many CBOs already use these tools very successfully. However, obstacles sometimes occur when CBOs operate on their instincts, rather than using more objective and structured tools to ensure their impact is as wide as possible. People expect CBOS to operate in a highly professional manner.

This notebook will help you and your CBO to ensure that you use these tools in the most effective way possible. We will look at advocacy, lobbying and communication as separate processes, but will also highlight the links between them. Often they are difficult to tell apart, but they need to work in harmony to ensure your campaigns are successful.

2. Advocacy

Advocacy means any action geared towards changing the policies, positions or programmes of any institution.

The first step is to identify a problem in a community. You need to understand all the aspects of the problem and find ways to help others to understand the problem fully. Then you can find ways to solve the issue.

Once everyone understands the issue clearly, you need to come up with a solution to that problem. You will need strong support for that solution and you will need an effective implementation plan to ensure your solution is correct.

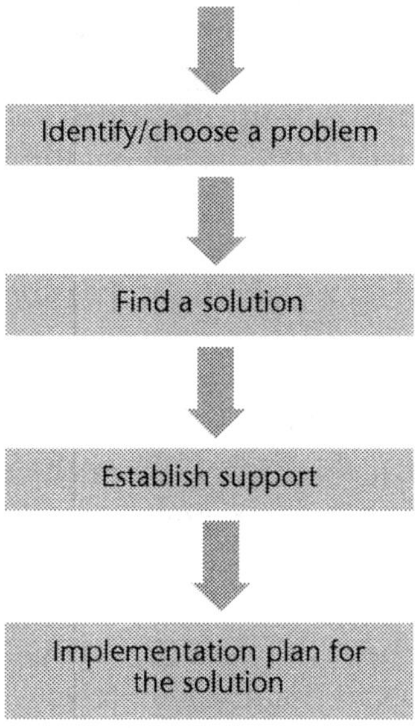

In essence advocacy is about coming up with an argument to support the position you hold. This position or opinion will be to solve a problem.

3. Lobbying

Lobbying is an attempt by citizens to influence others, particularly high-level public officials. Lobbying is one of the most common methods used by citizens to influence public policy. It enables citizens to put pressure on politicians and government officials so that they take an interest in the people and support their community's cause.

In most democracies lobbying is recognised as a legitimate way for citizens to make their voices heard. However, critics of lobbying say that wealthy people and businesses are better able to spend more time on – and pay for – various lobbying strategies and activities and therefore have greater influence with public officials than ordinary citizens.

You will find that lobbying requires some level of formality. One aspect of lobbying is, of course, building relationships with those people who can influence the advocacy campaign that you are about to run. However, when lobbying government it is not simply a matter of knowing the right people and phoning or meeting them to get their support. You will need to ensure you have covered the following aspects:

- Determine the facts;
- Get as many different opinions on the matter as possible;
- Decide on one viewpoint that you want to follow;
- Convince the decision-makers;
- Draw up a formal submission;

- Get your submission in on time; and
- Be proactive – don't wait for the deadline before you start the lobbying process.

4. Communication

You cannot run an advocacy campaign without good communication. Many campaigns often fail because the communication has not been clear or has not reached the people for whom it was intended. You must ensure that you use the appropriate method to communicate your message.

4.1. Understanding communication

Communication involves sharing an idea or concept with interested parties. This can involve communication between two people, or between organisations, or between one organisation and many people.

As in any process you will need to determine what your goal is. The possibilities might be:

- To inform;
- To persuade;
- To motivate; or
- To entice people into action.

4.2. Steps in the communication process

Communication is not just what one party wants to say to another. There are seven steps in the communication process. They are:

Step 1	Develop the idea you want to transmit;
Step 2	Convert the idea into suitable words or symbols for transmission;
Step 3	Transmit the idea by a method chosen, eg newsletter or meeting – make sure your message is appropriate for the receiver;
Step 4	Receiver gets the transmission;
Step 5	Receiver decodes the message – with luck exactly as it was sent and s/he understands it in the same way;
Step 6	Receiver accepts the message;
Step 7	Receiver uses the information – either by rejecting it or using it to act.

To ensure your communication is successful and strategic you should ask yourself the following questions:

- Which audiences do we need to reach?
- Have we conducted an audience analysis?
- What do we want people who hear our message to do?
- What messages could be appropriate?
- Which channels of communication would be most appropriate?
- How will the communication process be monitored and evaluated?

5. Running a campaign

A campaign includes all aspects of advocacy, lobbying and communication. To run a campaign you will need to follow a structured process. The following are the key steps to run any campaign:

5.1. Define your issue

Usually when you decide to run an advocacy campaign you need to think about your issue very specifically. If you decide to tackle crime in your area, for example, you need to think about which aspect of crime you want to address. It would not be effective to tackle crime in general because the issue is too extensive. It would be better to be more specific and tackle a particular crime issue. Don't try to tackle too many issues at once. This can be confusing for those who you are trying to influence. Research has shown that single-issue campaigns are more effective.

5.2. Understand your issue

Make sure you understand the issue thoroughly.

If it is the first time you are dealing with a particular issue, you need to ensure you have examined all the background information you might need.

A thorough understanding of the issue will help you to decide on which areas you need to focus your campaign.

To understand your issue thoroughly, you will need to research it. Your research will depend on the issue your campaign decides to tackle.

Research is helpful in a number of ways: It can be used to:

- Affect the changes that can be made in a policy process;
- Assist you to choose an advocacy goal;
- Influence decision-makers directly;
- Inform the media, public or other organisations and institutions – they also could influence decision-makers;
- Support an existing advocacy position;
- Help you to find out what counter-arguments you might come across during your campaign;
- Change perceptions that people might have of the issue or problem you are tackling;
- Challenge myths and assumptions;
- Confirm policy and programmes that are in place elsewhere that work well; and
- Help you to reconsider strategies that are not working during your campaign.

5.3. Define a campaign objective

It might sound simple to point out that your campaign should have an objective. However, your campaign objective should be simple and easily understandable by you, your organisation and the people you are trying to reach. You might find that, as you start working on your objective, it will need to be rewritten a number of times. This is a useful exercise because it will ensure that everyone in your CBO understands exactly what you are about to undertake.

It also will help you to choose the right strategies to use in your campaign.

An advocacy objective aims to CHANGE policies, programmes or positions of government, institutions or organisations.

It is about what YOU want to change, WHO will make the change, HOW and WHEN the change will take place.

All objectives should be SMART:

Specific
Measurable
Achievable
Realistic
Time-specific

If your campaign is not working as effectively as you had hoped, you might want consider revisiting your objective.

5.4. Choosing advocacy and lobbying strategies

There are many different strategies and tactics available to people planning to run a campaign. Your strategies must match your objective.

Example

You and your CBO have joined a number of organisations to advocate for a gun-free zone at your local high school. You decide to organise a barricade with burning tyres as part of your protest action against the number of assaults taking place at the school by young people carrying guns.

This strategy could work against you. Although you are trying to advocate an end to violence in schools, you are using violence yourself to achieve this. The result may be that people do not take you seriously.

The following table is a list of possible activities you could choose for your campaign instead. When you decide what action to take, you must ensure you have adequate resources from which to draw to implement your activity successfully.

Low-intensity activities	**Medium-intensity activities**	**High-intensity activities**
✧ Writing to an Member of Parliament (MP) or your local councillor ✧ Sending out media releases ✧ Doing media interviews ✧ Having lunch with the editor or a senior reporter of a local newspaper	✧ Producing a campaign newsletter ✧ Selling T-shirts, hats, badges and stickers to support the campaign ✧ Forming an alliance with a network of community organisations ✧ Paying for a newspaper advertisement ✧ Monitoring the local council ✧ Asking for a private meeting with the relevant councillor ✧ Persuading an opposition party councillor to ask a question at the council meeting ✧ Sending a written submission to the council ✧ Attracting the interest of an international non-governmental organisation (NGO), like Greenpeace	✧ Lobbying members of the ward committee ✧ Organising a mass picket or boycott ✧ Organising a one-day strike in support of the campaign ✧ Taking the council to court

The above activities fall into seven categories that make up the tools you have at your disposal to run your campaign. These categories are:

Information

Gathering, managing and disseminating the information you find lays the basis for determining the direction of an advocacy campaign. Research is one way to gather information.

Media

Various media can be used to communicate the campaign message to the different stakeholders.

Social mobilisation

Mobilising the broadest support from a range of stakeholders, including the public, is essential to building the influence of the campaign.

Lobbying

Convincing decision-makers who have the power to make the desired changes involves special knowledge and skills.

Litigation

Sometimes using the court system to challenge a policy or law can reinforce an advocacy campaign.

Networks, alliances and coalitions

Sharing information, resources and strengths in unity and commonality of purpose are key to the success of advocacy work.

Later in this notebook you will find an example that shows how, if planned and coordinated successfully, a campaign can use all of the tools in the toolkit.

It is important to remember that in a democratic society we might have to accept that we cannot win every campaign we pursue. There are limits to the actions we can take. If we have problems with some of the laws or regulations in our country, we should not undertake illegal action, such as burning buildings. You will be more successful if you use other avenues, such as lobbying, to change the laws and regulations.

5.5. Who are all the players and stakeholders?

Different players and/or stakeholders might require different strategies. The same strategy that you use to mobilise the youth in faith-based institutions will not be the same strategy you use to win over the local business community to your side.

The following list is the broad categories that you might need to target:

- Government;
- Civil society organisations;
- Union federations;
- Business;
- Faith-based institutions;
- The media; and
- The public.

You will not need to target all stakeholders or role players each time you run a campaign. You must decide who can help you the most to achieve the aims of your campaign.

You must decide who your primary audience is and which sectors are your secondary audience. The primary audience is usually made up of decision-makers who have the power to make the changes you would like to see take place. The secondary audience is made up of the people who will help you to bring pressure on the decision-makers.

Once you have decided on this you will need to 'unpack' each of the sectors. For example, you might find your primary audience is local government, but your secondary audience includes members of provincial and national government. You need to identify the specific players in each of the relevant spheres of government.

At a local government level you must decide if you should target the officials or the politicians? Do you need to target councillors from a particular sub-committee of council or only the chairperson of the sub-committee? If you want to target provincial government, have you decided to target officials or do you need to target the director-general or will the deputy director of a particular department be the best person?

If you want to target Muslim youth is it best to speak to the Imam at the mosque or should you contact a local Muslim youth civil society organisation?

Your understanding of power also influences your decisions about who the most appropriate person might be. For example, there might be a person in the opposition party who does not hold an elected position, but who might have a lot of power because s/he has been a member of the party for a long time and might have a good network system.

5.6. Planning the campaign

It is important to plan your campaign in as much detail as possible. There always will be unforeseen events that cannot be planned, but for those you can control, you should plan in detail.

You might have no financial resources for your campaign. If so, you might need to consider how you will recruit volunteers.

The *Project Management* notebook in this series will help you with the tools and techniques you need to plan effectively.

You might need to plan on an ongoing basis during your campaign because unexpected and unforeseen events unfold along the way. These might affect your campaign either positively or negatively and you have to learn how to deal with them.

When planning advocacy campaigns try to envisage all outcomes, good and bad. Try to have back-up strategies if one or more of your outcomes do not go according to plan.

5.7. Managing the campaign

It is a good idea to set up a team to coordinate the campaign. There should be no more than three 'captains' or 'managers' of the team.

The managing team should ensure that they set up project teams to manage various aspects of the campaign. Team members and managers will have different skills that will be useful when managing the various aspects of the campaign.

Depending on the nature of the campaign, there might have to be some degree of secrecy so that you can maintain an element of surprise. For example, if you are planning a sit-in at a local clinic, you do not want word to get out because managers of the clinic will do their best to ensure you do not gain entry into the clinic.

Generally, though, you will want as many people as possible to know about your activities so that they can join you and give their support. Your message will be more effective if you are open and transparent.

5.8. Communicating the campaign

There are five key areas to campaign communication:

Audience

Decide who your audience is and which strategy you need to communicate to that audience.

Desired action

You need to ask: what does our organisation want people to do when they get our message?

Take-away message

Good take-away messages focus on peoples' needs rather than on the needs of your organisation. You need to help

them to answer the question: what does this have to do with me? Try to ensure that you get the message across by using as many different channels as possible.

The message should be culturally sensitive. For example, if you are trying to convince older people to practise safe sex you will not be able to use the same message that you would use to convey the message to young people.

Channels

This refers to **how** you will deliver your message. Will you use meetings? Will you use radio or television or both? Will you use e-mail, newspapers, pamphlets, banners, etc? Supporting data will help – particularly if you need to do interviews on radio or TV, for example.

Evaluation

You need to ensure that you monitor the effect of your message in the community and on the role players and stakeholders constantly, so that you can see if you are targeting the correct audience. If it is not effective you might need to make changes. You also need to keep track of what methods work and those that don't, so that you can evaluate the campaign effectively.

The communication of your message, your successes and the need for other steps or activities will contribute to the campaign enormously. This is probably the most critical aspect of any campaign. If possible you should try to get the help of professionals or students in the field of communication because this could help you to get your message across more effectively.

5.9. Acknowledging contributors

People often work very hard to ensure a campaign is successful. Many are volunteers and give of their time freely with little personal compensation other than to see their principles and ideals achieved. Some donate money, services and/or goods. Donations often are the core to the success of any campaign. When the campaign is over you need to acknowledge the contributions of all the people involved. You might want to write a letter of thanks to individuals and organisations; you might consider inserting an advert in a local newspaper; or, if funds provide, you might hold a small party to thank participants.

Even if your campaign does not succeed, you need to acknowledge the contributions of all those involved. This simple step will encourage people to help the next time you run a campaign.

5.10. Evaluating the campaign

Evaluating the overall campaign is a critical step. There are many different tools in the evaluation process. Remember to document as much of your campaign as possible. It might be a good idea to have daily or weekly evaluation sessions, depending on the nature of your campaign. Write up all the lessons you learn so that the next time you and your organisation plan a campaign it will be as effective as possible.

6. Conclusion

The tools that are mentioned in this notebook should help you and your CBO to focus your attention and resources in a structured manner. It is our hope that your organisation will reap the benefits for both you and your community. Through strengthening the capacity and abilities of your CBO to advocate, lobby and communicate, we believe that democracy will be strengthened.

It is also critical that you consult some of the other notebooks in this series to enable you to run campaigns effectively, such as the *Project Management, Fundraising and Proposal Writing* and *CBOs and Mobilisation* notebooks. These will help you to run a well-resourced and well-managed campaign.

The key to all advocacy and lobbying initiatives is experience. You will make mistakes, but you will learn from them and the next campaign you tackle will go more smoothly.

Good luck! You will find that advocacy, lobbying and communication can be rewarding and exhilarating. You will achieve many objectives. And, as with all new skills, you will become better with time as you build up your network and learn from your mistakes and your successes.

7. References

Books

John W. Newstrom and Keith Davis. 2002. *Organisational Behaviour Human Behaviour at work.* McGraw-Hill Irwin Publishers. New York

Manuals

IDASA. 2004. *Advocacy & Communication*

IDASA. 2004. *How Local Government Works*

Websites

www.idasa.org.za

www.tac.org.za

FINANCIAL MANAGEMENT FOR COMMUNITY-BASED ORGANISATIONS

1. Introduction

Finding and keeping money is one of the most difficult tasks for any community-based organisation (CBO). Not only must CBOs be concerned with where they are going to get money, they must also be concerned with how that money is used once they get it. The management of the CBO must make sure that there is always strict control of the finances, otherwise the organisation runs the risk of not being able to do what it had planned or, even worse, of getting into financial trouble. This knowledge of and control over the finances of the organisation is called financial management.

The most important reason for financial management in any organisation is to ensure that the organisation knows how much money it needs, how to get the money it needs and then how to use that money to achieve its goals in an ethical, responsible and sustainable way. It is impossible for an organisation to survive without proper financial management.

An important element to remember is that unless the CBOs use their money in an open and accountable way, there is a good chance that they will not receive money from donors. Donors want to know that their money is being well spent and that will happen only if there is strong financial management in the organisation being funded. Strong financial management structures make it much easier for an organisation to report back to its donors and this gives the donors confidence in the management of the organisation. Donors will, obviously, rather give money to organisations that they trust than to those they don't.

Financial management is a job and a responsibility that involves the past, the present and the future. Firstly, proper financial management means that you have to keep a record of all the money that your organisation has already received or spent (the past). Secondly, you must control and manage the money that is still in the organisation (present) and finally, financial management helps you to make decisions about the future of the organisation. Proper financial management helps the management of the organisation to plan for the future, because it tells the management how much money it has, how much money it needs and what its plans for the future will cost.

To look after the past, present and future finances of your organisation means that financial management involves three different, but connected, jobs. They are:

- Financial planning (future);
- Financial control (present); and
- Financial monitoring (past).

To make these three jobs more understandable, this notebook starts with the broad concepts and then takes a look at each of the different jobs in more detail. It is, however, important to remember that the main goal of this notebook is to give a general idea of what financial management is and why it is important to a business or organisation. If possible, however, it is always advisable for an organisation to employ a qualified bookkeeper, either part-time or full-time, who already has a good understanding of the principles and responsibilities of financial management.

2. What is financial management?

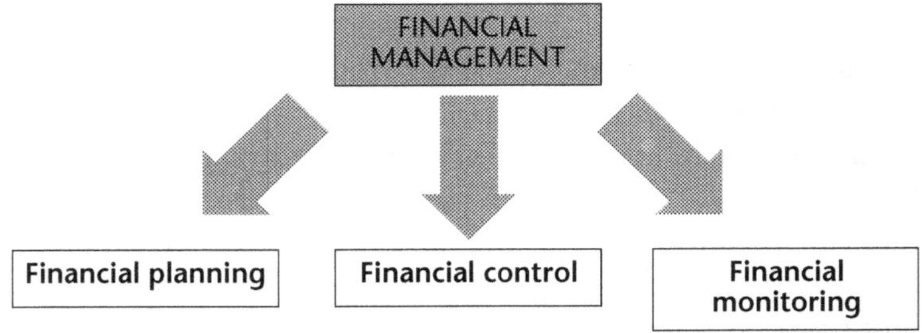

Financial management is based on two very important principles:

- **Financial responsibility:** You should always try to manage your finances in a responsible and sustainable way. All organisations need money to survive and achieve their goals. The only way they can ensure this is to manage their money in such a way that they don't put the organisation in unnecessary danger. If an organisation plans to exist in the future, it must make sure that it receives enough money and then spends it wisely.
- **Financial accountability:** The organisation must be able to account for where its money comes from and the way the money is spent. Accountability not only helps you to keep track of what has been done with the money, it also allows you to explain your activities to your stakeholders. This is particularly important for CBOs and other organisations that need donor funds, because in most cases donors have strict rules and requirements for accountability. They will only fund organisations that can account for the money that they have received.

Through proper financial management, you identify what you want to do, what you can do, how much money you have, how much money you need, how your money has been spent and where you can get more money. This process involves three activities:

- **Planning:** Helps you to identify what the organisation's future goals are, how much money you will need to achieve these goals and how or where you will find enough money to achieve these goals and keep the organisation going in the future.
- **Controlling:** Involves several different steps:
  1. *Determining Policy:* The organisation must decide what rules and procedures must be followed to ensure that its money is spent properly and safely;
  2. *Determining delegated powers:* The organisation must decide who will be allowed to spend money, how much they will be allowed to spend and when will they be allowed to spend it. It is important also to decide who can make financial commitments on behalf of the organisations;
  3. *Determining responsibility:* The goal here is to decide who is responsible for the organisation's money. It is important that a specific person – or people – takes responsibility for the organisation's money. Not everyone can be in charge of the finances.
- **Monitoring:** This activity involves:
  1. Recording financial information – bookkeeping;
  2. Preparing financial statements;
  3. Analysing financial statements; and
  4. Financial reporting.

3. Financial planning

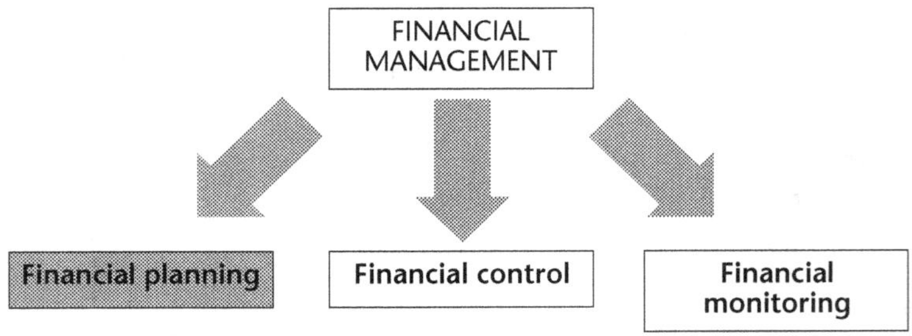

Financial planning is a process that an organisation uses to work out what resources it has available, what resources it needs and where extra resources can be found. The most important tools for financial planning are the financial strategy and the budget. The difference between the tools is that the budget usually concerns shorter-term planning, while the financial strategy is more concerned with the medium- to long-term needs of the organisation.

3.1 Financial strategy

The purpose of a financial strategy is to ensure that an organisation knows what its financial needs are and where it will get the necessary funding to meet those needs. In general, this has to do with the medium- and long-term financial needs of the organisation.

When you sit down to do your financial strategy, you should not think only about finding money for immediate projects or for this year's budget, you also have to consider ways to secure the medium- to long-term financial future of the organisation. In short, you must make sure that there is money available for the present and the future.

When you work on your financial strategy, remember to examine ways to make more money, as well as ways to spend less money. On the one hand, you must look for new ways to bring money into the organisation, while on the other hand, you must look at ways to limit or cut the amount of money you are already spending.

3.1.1 Ways to increase income

- **Donors:** For most CBOs the first source of funding that comes to mind is donors. In many cases it is the only source of funding that comes to mind. Some organisations get lucky and find a donor that is willing and able to provide enough money for most of the organisation's expenses, but that usually does not happen. In most cases even the most dedicated donors are not able to provide all the money an organisation needs. Donors also might not be able to provide money for a long period of time. Nevertheless, donor funding remains one of the most important sources of funding for CBOs and it should be considered the first option when an organisation is looking for money.

  It is always advisable to get more than one donor. In this way you are able to spread the burden among a group of donors instead of relying only on one. In the case of CBOs, there is funding available not only from foreign or international donors, but also from local or provincial government. At provincial level these funds are usually disbursed by departments such as social development or welfare, while at local level they are disbursed by the local council or municipality. It is, therefore, important for CBOs to approach their local and provincial governments as a first port of call, especially if their activities are aligned to the priorities of the respective government structures.

- **Internal income generation:** Internal income generation means that the organisation makes its own money. There are many ways that an organisation can make money. An organisation can, for example, charge a fee for some of the work it does. The money it makes can be used for other projects or activities. Some specific income-generating options include:
    - Asking for contributions from members;
    - Selling goods and merchandise like publications, T-shirts, etc;
    - Selling certain services;
    - Providing training to other people or organisations;
    - Doing project management for other people;
    - Providing managerial services;
    - Providing secretarial services; and
    - Earning interest on the organisation's investments.

3.1.2 Ways to reduce expenditure

Apart from finding sources of income, financial strategies must include expenditure. The aim of an expenditure strategy is to see how you can spend less money, while at the same time continuing to do the same amount of work or even more work. There are several factors worth considering:

- **Cutting services:** It is sometimes necessary for an organisation to cut some of its services when it sees that the impact of the service does not justify the amount of money being spent on it;
- **Outsourcing:** It is sometimes cheaper to get someone from outside the organisation to do a specific task than it is to employ a full-time worker to do it;

- **Full utilisation of staff time:** This means that the management must ensure that all of the employees are being used to their full capacity. An organisation wastes a lot of money if its employees are being paid, but not being used all of the time;
- **Cheaper suppliers:** Try to find suppliers who can provide products or services at a cheaper price than the rest. In most cases this involves some shopping around or negotiating for the best price;
- **Cheaper rent:** One of the biggest expenses for most organisations is the rent they have to pay for their offices. Therefore, it is important to try to find the cheapest possible office space that still meets the needs of the organisation; and
- **Monitor expenses:** Management must always monitor all expenses to make sure that the organisation's money is not being abused or wrongly spent. Some expenses, such as telephone accounts, can get out of control quickly if someone does not monitor them carefully to ensure that people are not making unnecessary phone calls.

3.1.3 Financial planning steps

The development of an effective strategic financial plan involves the following basic steps:

- **Set medium- to long-term goals and objectives for the organisation:** These goals must be stated in figures, for example, the number of projects you want to run or the number of programmes you want to launch. Now you can use these figures to work out exactly what resources will be required;
- **Develop medium- to long-range implementation plans:** This will enable you to attain your goals and objectives. Here you must think of everything inside

and outside the organisation that might influence your ability to achieve your goals. Once you are certain that you have thought of all the possible problems and challenges, you must develop strategies or plans that will help you to achieve your goals and overcome the challenges;

- **Determine the financial, human, and physical requirements necessary to achieve your plan**: In other words, work out exactly how many resources you will need to make your plan work. You must also work out how much money you will need for each of the plans that you develop;
- **Develop concrete income and expenditure plans**: Write down exactly how you plan to meet the financial needs of your strategy. This includes identifying ways to increase your income or to decrease your expenses; and
- **Revise, revise and revise**: Once your strategy is in place, don't be afraid of changing your plans if you realise that you are not able to find enough money or if you get more money than you expected.

3.2 Budget

The budget is the most important financial planning tool of an organisation. The budget comes directly from the activity objectives or outputs of the organisation. It shows what the organisation expects its activities to cost during a specific time period. The difference between the budget and the strategic financial plan is that the budget uses actual existing figures. In other words, the budget is based on the actual amount of money that an organisation expects to get and that it expects to spend. It is not only a strategy to help manage your income or to cut expenses; it shows the actual situation for a given time period.

The difficulty with budgeting is that the finances of the whole organisation can depend on the accuracy of a budget. If the budget is too low, the organisation might not be able to meet its financial commitments or deliver the desired outcomes. If the budget is too high, there is a risk that funders might not be interested in funding the project or organisation.

In general there are three different types of budgets:

- Firstly, there is an *operating budget* (or annual budget), which shows how much money will be needed over a longer period, such as year or for the duration of a specific project or programme. Budget amounts are usually divided into major categories (salaries, benefits, computer equipment, office supplies), but these major categories can be divided into smaller, very specific items if needed. The more detailed the categories the more accurate the budget;
- Secondly, there are *cash budgets* that show the amount of cash you expect to receive and pay in the near term, for example, a month; and
- Finally, you might have *capital budgets*, which show how much money you have to spend if you want to buy, operate and maintain major pieces of equipment, for example, buildings, cars, computers, furniture, etc.

Depending on the size of the organisation, it might be necessary to prepare all the different types of budgets for each of the big services or programmes that you provide to your clients. Many non-profit organisations or CBOs have more than one programme or project that they are involved in and it is important to budget for each of these activities.

Usually, each month you have to update your budget report so that it shows the money that has already come in or that has already been spent. This helps the organisation to see if it is still on target or whether it is spending too much or receiving too little. This gives you a good idea of whether you are working according to plan and whether you need to cut expenses and build up income.

3.2.1 The budgeting process

The first step in any budgeting process is to make sure that you know exactly what you are budgeting for. In other words, it is important for the person or people doing the budget to know exactly what the activity or activities are that are being budgeted for.

Once you know what will be done, you have to find out all the possible areas of expenditure. These are called the expenditure line items in your budget. Each different type of expense becomes a different line item. An example could be a line item for transport and a line item for salaries. It is important that *every single expense* is shown in the budget as a line item.

Once the different (expenditure) items have been identified, it is necessary to identify the different income items. List all your sources of income.

Next you must work out exactly how much money will be needed for each expenditure item and how much money will be received from each income item. These figures must be as accurate as possible, because often they cannot be changed once the project has begun. These amounts must be used to establish if there is enough money coming in to cover the amount of money that will be going out. If there is not enough, the expenses must be reduced or extra income must be found.

Once you have finalised your income and expenditure budgets, it is important to work out a cash flow budget based on those figures. The cash flow budget not only shows the amount of income and expenditure, it also adds a time element to the income and expenditure. In other words, the cash flow budget not only shows how much money will come in and go out, it also shows when the money will come in or go out. This is important because you have to make sure that your income and expenses are co-ordinated. For instance, you cannot start spending money if you have not yet received any money.

Budgeting checklist

Step 1: Plan your activities for the period in question;
Step 2: Work out what your different expenditure items will be;
Step 3: Work out what your different income items will be;
Step 4: Find out exactly what each of your expenditure items will cost;
Step 5: Work out exactly what your income will be;
Step 6: Work out if there is any shortfall between income and expenditure;
Step 7: From your income and expenditure budget, work out a cash flow budget;
Step 8: Present your draft budgets for comments;
Step 9: Change your budgets if needed; and
Step 10: Finalise your income and expenditure budgets and cash flow budget.

Example: *Project budget*

Income		
Donations	500 000	
Internal income	50 000	
Interest	20 000	
Total income		**570 000**
Expenditure		
Salaries	350 000	
Printing and stationery	100 000	
Telephone and fax	50 000	
Rent	50 000	
Venue hire	30 000	
Total expenditure		**580 000**
Excess/(deficit)		**(10 000)**

4. Financial control

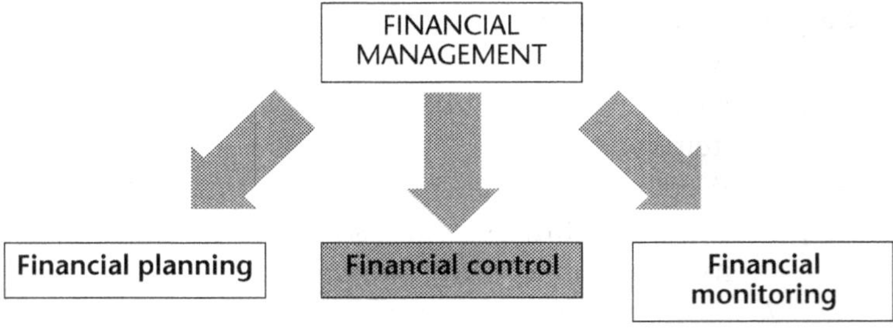

Financial control involves two elements. Firstly, it deals with the issue of financial responsibility within an organisation and, secondly, it deals with the issue of decision-taking and implementation. In every organisation there are different levels of financial control. This ensures that specific people are responsible for all the organisation's finances. It also establishes the practical financial rules, policies and procedures that are used in the organisation to make sure that it continues to function properly.

Financial responsibility in most organisations takes place at different levels. The first level of control is generally financial responsibility for all finances. This is usually at the board or senior management level. These people are usually directly involved in making financial policy, ensuring that the financial policy is being used, making sure that budgets are realistic and meet the goals of the organisation, and ensuring that spending is monitored and that organisational assets are protected. They also bear the ultimate responsibility for all financial matters

The second level is a delegated level, which is concerned with the day-to-day management of financial affairs. These are the people who apply policy, authorise expenditure, prepare and monitor the budget and make financial proposals. Financial planning means nothing if the staff members of the organisation do not have the ability to implement the plans and to take decisions about them. This includes the ability to spend money and to make financial decisions.

Financial control, therefore, refers to all of the processes, procedures and policies that are put in place to ensure that money is spent in the right way and that the goals and objectives of the organisation are met and achieved through this expenditure. This level of financial control can be achieved through both internal and external controls.

4.1 Internal control

The aim of an internal control structure is to ensure that the organisation achieves all its goals. In designing an internal control structure you must ensure that it does not become too expensive. It would not make sense to have expensive and complicated internal controls for an organisation with a small and uncomplicated budget.

Effective and efficient internal controls should maintain reliable financial records, protect the assets of the organisation, authorise transactions and provide accountability. There are many different forms of internal control, but two of the most important are discussed below.

4.1.1 Accounting and financial procedures manual

One of the most common and useful forms of internal financial control is an accounting procedures manual. This document is a record of the policies and procedures for handling financial transactions. The manual describes in detail how the organisation's money must be handled (for example, paying bills, depositing cash and transferring money between funds) and who is responsible for what. The accounting procedures manual is also useful when there is a change-over in financial management staff.

4.1.2 Delegation of responsibility

In most small organisations, delegation of financial responsibility is not a problem because one or two people are responsible for everything. In larger organisations this becomes very important, because the functioning of the organisation depends on a large group of people being able to work independently of one another. For this to happen a certain amount of delegation of financial control is required. It is almost impossible to implement a project if the implementer has no financial control. The level of control that is given to the implementer can, however, differ from organisation to organisation, person to person and project to project. The important element is that all of the people in the organisation must know exactly what they can or cannot do in terms of finances and there must be clarity on who will take final responsibility for the finances of the organisation.

4.2 External control

4.2.1 External audit

Another form of financial control is an audit. An audit is a comprehensive analysis, by a professional from outside the organisation, of the organisation's financial management procedures and activities. The auditor produces a report that shows how well the organisation is managing its resources. Some non-profit organisations are required to have audits. It's usually good practice to have an audit, whether it's required or not. In the case of small CBOs there is no need for an external audit because the amount of money being managed does not justify the cost of an audit.

5. Financial monitoring

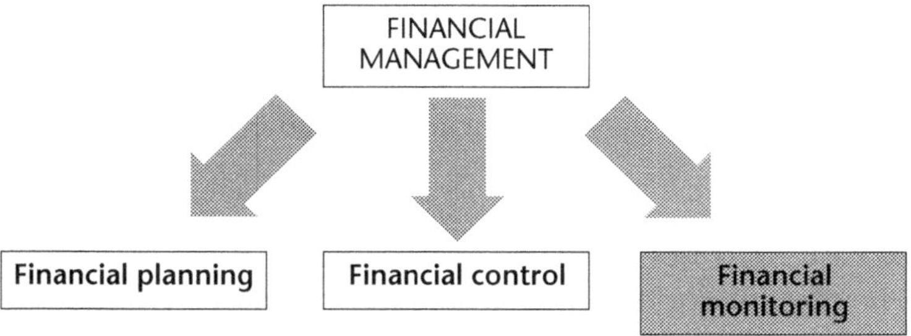

The final activity in the financial management process involves recording, analysing and reporting on the finances of the organisation. This is without any doubt the most time-consuming and labour-intensive activity in the financial management process because it is a never-ending and ongoing activity.

The basic reason for financial monitoring is to help the management of the organisation to plan and control the finances. To plan and control finances there has to be accurate and up-to-date information available on the financial position of an organisation at any given time. This is achieved firstly by recording every single activity that involves the money of the organisation; secondly, by analysing the information in the record; and thirdly, by providing the information in the records to the relevant stakeholders in the form of financial reports so that they can use the information to plan and control the organisation's finances. Planning and control would be impossible without the information that management gets from these reports.

The following sections provide a broad overview of the different elements of financial monitoring, as well as an overview of the different elements that the management of a CBO would have to consider and/or make decisions about. This is not a comprehensive manual on accounting or bookkeeping and therefore it is important to remember that, if at all possible, a full- or part-time bookkeeper, who already has the relevant training, should be employed by the organisation.

5.1 Record keeping/bookkeeping

The most important element of financial monitoring is access to accurate and up-to-date information. Every single financial transaction must be recorded for this to happen. In other words, every cent that comes into the organisation and every cent that goes out of the organisation must be recorded. This is commonly known as bookkeeping. The purpose of any bookkeeping system is to record all the events that take place in an organisation. In accounting terms these events are called transactions.

5.1.1 Accounting systems

Cash-basis accounting/chequebook accounting: When your organisation is just getting started, your bookkeeping system will probably be based on what's called a cash-basis accounting system. Many organisations, when starting out, use the cash-basis system and a chequebook to keep track of their transactions. The cash-basis system works on actual income and expenses, which means that you add or subtract money from your account only once it has actually been deposited or withdrawn.

When this system is combined with a chequebook system, the 'memo' portion of the chequebook is used to keep track of all the money that comes into or goes out of the organisation. In practical terms this means that you must write down every single transaction in the 'memo' portion of the chequebook and then you must either add or subtract those amounts from the balance in the chequebook.

Smaller organisations, which work with small amounts of money, usually find it easier to keep track of financial activity by running all of their financial transactions through a single cheque account. Very small organisations, with few deposits and expenses, can even prepare reports directly from the chequebook after the chequebook balance has been reconciled with the bank balance. This means that they should check regularly to ensure that the amount of money in the bank account is the same as the amount of money that the chequebook says they should have.

However, as organisations grow, they begin to earn and spend more money and eventually it becomes difficult to keep track of the money using only a chequebook. At this point the organisation has to start using journals and ledgers to track transactions; for example, cash payments will be recorded in a cash receipts journal and check payments in a cash disbursements journal.

Accrual-basis accounting: In an accrual-basis system you record transactions when you earn the money and when you owe it. In other words, you do not wait until the money is actually deposited or withdrawn. This differs from cash-basis accounting because you record the transaction even before the actual money has been paid or received. A good example would be your electricity account. In cash-basis accounting you would record the transaction only once you have actually paid, but in the accrual-basis system you record the transaction as soon as you receive the bill, even before it has actually been paid.

Small organisations usually do not have the resources to use an accrual-based system. However, financial statements are prepared on an accrual basis. As a compromise, many organisations use the cash-based basis to record entries in journals, but get help from a part-time bookkeeper or accountant to convert to an accrual-based basis to generate financial statements.

As an organisation grows and begins using the accrual method, it will likely need more types of journals, for example, a cash receipts journal, cash disbursements journal, payroll journal, accounts receivable ledger, accounts payable ledger, sales journal, purchases journal and general ledger. Each journal is used to record a specific activity. Instead of recording everything in one journal, activities are recorded in different journals. At this point it is advisable that a bookkeeper be employed.

5.1.2 Single-entry or double-entry accounting method

Single-entry method: The single-entry method of recording financial activity is usually used by small organisations which do not manage a lot of money. The single-entry method is usually part of a chequebook accounting system. In a single-entry system you keep track only of the difference between the money received and the money spent. Unfortunately, you need extra information to make good financial decisions. For example, you have to know how much your equipment is worth, how much you have, how much money you are owed and how much money you owe. With this system, you have to keep separate records for all these aspects as well, because they are not part of your accounting system. In small organisations this is fine, but in larger organisations this creates a lot of extra work.

Double-entry method: Double-entry accounting works from the following basic accounting equation:
'Assets = Liabilities + Capital'

The double-entry method makes sure that your books are always in balance. Every transaction has two journal entries, a debit and a credit. Each transaction affects both sides of the equation. In simple terms this means that every entry that is done in one journal also has an entry in another journal or if you take from one account you add to another. In practical terms there are nine possible entries that can be made using the accounting equation shown above:

1. One asset account is debited and another asset account credited;
2. One liability account is debited and another liability account credited;
3. One capital account is debited and another capital account is credited;
4. A capital account is debited and a liability account is credited;

5. A capital account is debited and an asset account is credited;
6. A capital account is credited and a liability account is debited;
7. A capital account is credited and an asset account is debited;
8. An asset account is debited and a liability account is credited; and
9. An asset account is credited and a liability account is debited.

An example of how this works is when you pay an account. According to this method of accounting you have to record that your accounts payable journal has been credited and that your bank account has been debited. This shows that money has been taken from your bank account and that money has been paid into your accounts payable account. If you make only one journal entry, there will be an error in your financial records. If you don't make the bank account entry, your bank balance will be too high. If you don't make the accounts payable entry, your total debt (liabilities) will be more than it actually is. The advantage of this method is the fact that your overall financial position is continuously updated. Unlike the single-entry system, you don't need extra records to keep track of your debts or inventories. All the aspects of your finances are already part of this method.

Whether you use a single or a double-entry method, it is extremely important that each transaction that is recorded should refer to supporting documents that you keep in a file somewhere. For example, postings about cash receipts might refer to invoices that you sent to clients which prompted them to write cheques to your organisation (cheques which you posted as cash receipts). In another example, postings about cash disbursements might refer to invoices that were sent to your organisation which prompted you to write cheques (cheques which you posted as cash disbursements). When you make a deposit to the bank, you'll file the bank's deposit receipt in a file. These documents help you to explain your activities and to support your bookkeeping entries.

5.1.3 Manual/computer-based accounting

Your record keeping/bookkeeping system will be based on either a manual system or a computerised/automated system. A manual accounting system records and processes accounting information by hand, while an automated accounting system uses computers to record and process financial information. It is important to remember that the way in which an accounting system works basically stays the same in both systems. The computerised system just makes it easier to record and save large amounts of information.

At the start you might use a manual system because of the few entries that have to be captured but, as your organisation grows, you might have to evolve to using a computer-based system, which makes it easier and quicker to enter transactions, update ledgers and to generate financial statements. It also makes financial analysis and the generation of financial reports a lot easier.

The only drawback to using a computer is that you might underestimate the importance of knowing how your accounting processes really work – that is an advantage to doing the bookkeeping yourself, if only for a few months. You also should generate your own financial statements and financial analysis at least for a couple of months. Having this knowledge and experience helps you to develop an instinct for getting the most out of your financial resources.

5.1.4 Bookkeeping activities

The job of the bookkeeper is one of routine. This job can be divided into three types of activities. Business transactions are collected and recorded on a daily basis, collated and summarised on a monthly basis and processed at year-end to determine the financial success or failure of the organisation. What follows is a more in-depth discussion of the tasks and responsibilities during each of these activities.

Daily

Task 1: Daily transactions include buying, selling, collecting money from debtors, paying regular expenses, etc. All of these activities must be recorded by the bookkeeper so that there is a record of what has happened to the organisation's money. As such, the first task of the bookkeeper is to record these transactions on their source documents in written form. This means that a special document should be designed for each of the different types of transaction and each transaction is then recorded by filling in the right type of document.

Task 2: At the end of each day the information for that day, which has been recorded on the source documents, must be sorted and the information recorded in a transaction journal. The journals are the different record-keeping books that are used to record transactions. This could include a cash payments book or a cash receipts book, or a debtors' book or a creditors' book. In small organisations this could mean that each of the different transactions is recorded in the memo section of the chequebook.

Monthly activities

Task 1: The main monthly activity is to consolidate (add together) all the information in the different journals into a single record, called a ledger. The ledger is divided into a nominal and balance sheet section. The nominal section is the record of all the money that has actually come in or gone out, while the balance sheet section shows how the income or expenditure has influenced the actual financial position of the organisation.

Task 2: Once the journals have been consolidated, the ledger accounts are balanced and a trial balance is drawn up. Balancing accounts refers to making sure that the information in the different journals was correctly transferred to the ledger. Once the ledger has been created, all of the information in it must match the journals exactly.

Task 3: Account statements are sent to debtors. At the end of each month the bookkeeper must send accounts to everyone who owes the organisation money.

Task 4: Payments are made to creditors. The bookkeeper must ensure that the organisation pays all of its debts at the end of the month.

Task 5: The creditors' ledger, the debtors' ledger and the bank statements are reconciled. In doing this the bookkeeper must ensure that all the payments made and all the payments received are recorded in the creditors' and debtors' journals and he/she must make sure that the money has actually been deposited into or been withdrawn from the bank account.

Annual/yearly activities

Task 1: All inventories are checked and the inventory account is adjusted to reflect any surpluses or shortages. If the organisation sells products to make money, it is important to see how much of the product is still available. This is important for two reasons. Firstly, you can see whether the amount of product that is left matches your records and you can adjust your records in line with what is actually available. Secondly, it helps prevent theft, because everyone knows that the products are counted and that there are records of how much should be available.

Task 2: Adjustments are made to the nominal accounts to reflect accruals, deferments or depreciation. This means the income and expenditure accounts are changed because the original entries are no longer right.

Task 3: Nominal accounts are closed off to the two final accounts, namely the trading account and the profit and loss account. At this point all the information in the different nominal accounts is combined into two accounts.

Task 4: Total surpluses or deficits are calculated. By using the trading and profit and loss accounts, you can see if the organisation has made or lost money during the year and you can work out exactly how much was made or lost.

Task 5: The information in the trading and profit and loss accounts is used to prepare the final income statement and balance sheet. These two reports give an overview of exactly what the organisation's financial position is at that specific point in time.

Task 6: The financial results and reports are reviewed by the management.

5.2 Preparation of financial statements

To evaluate your organisation, you have to do ongoing financial planning and analysis. In this planning and analysis you'll have to use your bookkeeping information to produce different kinds of financial statements, including a cash flow statement, statement of activities and a statement of financial position. These financial statements record the performance of your business and allow you to see what its strengths and weaknesses are by providing a written summary of financial activities. The two most important and most used financial statements are the balance sheet and the income statement.

5.2.1 The balance sheet

The balance sheet gives an overall picture of the financial situation of an organisation at a given moment, usually at the end of an accounting period. It lists in detail everything that the organisation owns (known as its assets), as well as everything that the organisation owes.

Assets include not only cash, merchandise, land, buildings, equipment, machinery, furniture, patents, trademarks and the like, but also money that is owed to the organisation by other organisations or people (known as accounts or notes receivable).

Liabilities are the money or items that the organisation owes to other organisations or people. This can include money that is loaned to the organisation or any products or services that the organisation has bought on credit. A good example of this would be money that is owed to a bank after your organisation borrows money to buy office equipment. The amount that is still owed to the bank at a given time will always appear on the balance sheet as a liability. It is important to note that liabilities do not refer to short-term debt, such as your electricity account; it refers only to debt that must be paid back over a longer period.

At any given time an organisation's assets will equal its total liabilities, plus the total amount of money that has been put into the organisation by its funders or members.

The balance sheet is designed to show how the assets, liabilities and capital are distributed at any given time. It is usually prepared at regular intervals; for example, at each month's end, but especially at the end of each fiscal (accounting) year.

By regularly preparing this summary of what the organisation owns and owes (the balance sheet), the management can identify and analyse trends in the financial strength of the business. It also gives a good idea of what the management needs to do to improve its financial position, such as gradually decreasing the amount of money the organisation owes to creditors.

All balance sheets contain the same categories of assets, liabilities and capital. Assets are arranged in decreasing order of how quickly they can be turned into cash (liquidity). Liabilities are listed in order of how soon they must be repaid, followed by retained earnings (money that can be kept in the organisation).

The categories and format of the balance sheet are established by a system known as *generally accepted accounting principles* (GAAP). The system is applied to all organisations, large or small, so anyone reading the balance sheet can understand the story it tells.

Balance sheet categories: Assets and liabilities are broken down into categories as described below:

Assets: an asset is anything the business owns that has monetary value.

- *Current assets* include cash, money that has been invested in securities, accounts receivable, notes receivable, inventories, prepaid expenses and any other item that could be converted into cash within one year in the normal course of business;
- *Fixed assets* are those acquired for long-term use in a business, such as land, plant, equipment, machinery, leasehold improvements, furniture, fixtures and any other items with an expected useful business life measured in years;
- *Other assets* include intangible assets, such as patents, royalty arrangements, copyrights, exclusive use contracts and notes receivable from officers and employees.

Liabilities: are the claims of creditors against the assets of the business (debts owed by the business).

- *Current liabilities* are accounts payable, notes payable to banks, accrued expenses (wages, salaries), taxes payable, the current portion (due within one year) of long-term debt and other obligations to creditors due within one year;
- *Long-term liabilities* are mortgages, intermediate and long-term bank loans, equipment loans and any other money due with a maturity longer than a year.

Capital: equals the assets of the organisation minus its liabilities.

Example: Typical balance sheet

Assets	Liabilities
Current assets	*Current liabilities*
✧ Cash	✧ Accounts payable
✧ Securities	✧ Accrued expenses
✧ Inventories, etc	✧ Current portion of long-term debt, etc
Fixed assets	*Long-term liabilities*
✧ Property	✧ Mortgages
✧ Machinery	✧ Long-term bank loans
✧ Furniture, etc	✧ Taxes payable
Other assets	
✧ Royalties	
✧ Copyright, etc	
	Capital

5.2.2 The income statement

The second primary report included in a financial statement is the income statement. The income statement measures the amount of money that has come into the organisation and that has been paid out by the organisation over a specific period of time. It is prepared regularly (each month and fiscal year-end) to show operating results during these accounting periods. It follows generally accepted accounting principles (GAAP) and contains specific income and expense categories regardless of the nature of the business.

Income statement categories: The income statement categories are calculated as described below:

- **Net income** (total income less any money that had to be returned);
- Less **cost of goods sold** (cost of inventories) – if the organisation sells goods;
- Equals **gross margin** (gross profit on sales before operating expenses);

- Less **administrative expenses** (salaries, wages, payroll taxes and benefits, rent, utilities, maintenance expenses, office supplies, postage, automobile/vehicle expenses, insurance, legal and accounting expenses, depreciation);
- Equals **operating profit** (profit before other non-operating income or expense);
- Plus **other income** (income from discounts, investments, customer charge accounts);
- Less **other expenses** (interest expense);
- Equals **net profit (or loss) before tax** (the figure on which your tax is calculated);
- Less **income taxes** (if any are due);
- Equals **net profit (or loss) after tax.**

5.3 Financial analysis

By themselves figures usually don't mean much. But, when you compare them with certain other numbers, you can learn a lot about how your organisation is doing. For example, you can compare the planned expenses depicted on your budget with your actual expenses to see if your spending is on track.

Another form of comparison is by using ratios. A ratio is a comparison made by dividing one figure by the other. For example, non-profit organisations are expected to keep administrative costs down to make more money available for programmes. Dividing a programme's expenses by your total expenses indicates the amount of administrative overheads to run your programme. If you do this exercise regularly, you will see quickly if the amount you are spending on administrative overheads is staying level or if it is going up or down.

The interpretation of results from various types of comparisons depends on the nature of the organisation.

For example, an association might expect to spend far less on administrative overheads in its first year than social services agency would. The exact nature of the information you need from the analysis depends on the type of organisation that you are managing, as well as on the specific goals of the organisation.

5.4 Financial reporting

The types and frequency of reports depend on the nature of the organisation and its situation. For example, if the organisation is in some sort of financial crisis, the board or management might require frequent reports.

Your senior management or board should, however, require regular financial reports at each meeting. When your organisation is just getting started, the executive director will usually prepare and present financial reports to the board. However, as the organisation develops, a treasurer or financial manager will be appointed to help the executive director present financial information to the board. A finance committee, led by the financial manager, will often be created to make sure that financial reports are complete and to present them to other members of the board.

In general, the board will be interested in receiving reports on the current financial position of the organisation, the future activities of the organisation, details about the finance of each programme or project, as well as information on the organisation's taxes. These reports can all be done by using the information in the financial statements and analyses.

Apart from internal reporting, there is also a responsibility for CBOs to provide narrative and financial reports to their respective funders. Each funder has its own criteria for what the reports should look like and what they should contain, but in general there are two important elements that are required by all donors. Firstly, they require a narrative report that explains exactly what happened during the project and contains an analysis of whether the project achieved what was planned. In other words, they want to know they received value for their money. Secondly, all funders require a financial report at the end of each project in which the CBO must explain exactly how the money was used. Not only must the CBO report on how the funds were spent, they must also provide invoices and receipts for every single cent that was spent.

Reporting to the funders differs from reporting to the board of the organisation in that the funder reports are concerned with a specific project and a specific amount of money. The reports to the board are concerned with the overall financial welfare of the organisation.

The full picture

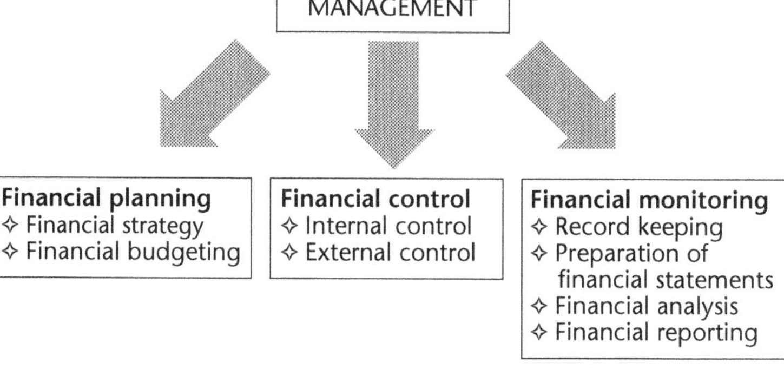

Glossary of Terms

Accounting system: The overall procedure of recording, classifying, sorting and summarising information and then later communicating that information.

Credit: The right-hand side of a ledger account. To credit an account means to record an entry on the right-hand side of an account. To sell something on credit means to sell on account, which also means to sell now and to pay at a later date.

Creditors: People or organisations to which you owe money.

Debit: The left-hand side of a ledger account. To debit an account means to record an entry on the left-hand side of an account.

Debtors: People or organisations that owe you money.

Journals: This is where transactions are recorded for the first time and sorted into similar transactions.

Ledger: A collection of accounts that are divided into the nominal and balance sheet sections.

Balance sheet accounts: These are the accounts that contain asset and liability accounts.

Nominal accounts: These are the accounts containing profit (income) and loss (expense) accounts.

Trial balance: A list of ledger account balances, usually drawn up at the end of the month.

Posting: Writing a transaction in one of the journals.

FUNDRAISING AND PROPOSAL WRITING

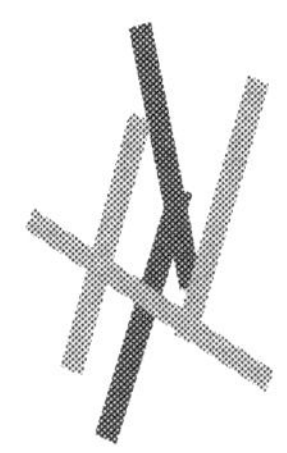

1. Overview

Most community-based organisations (CBOs) and other non-profit organisations depend on donors to provide money to run their organisations and projects. Unfortunately, there is lots of competition for donor money and in many cases the survival of an organisation depends on how well it can compete with other organisations to raise funds and on how good it is at finding other ways to make money.

Fundraising can be done in many ways, from collecting and selling cans, to cake sales to requesting large amounts of money from governments, individuals and other donor organisations. The list below gives a summary of the most important sources of large-scale funding:

- Individuals;
- Local businesses, companies and corporations;
- Special government funds, such as the Independent Development Trust (IDT);
- Provincial and local government departments;
- Local trusts and foundations;
- Foreign governments;
- Foreign non-governmental organisations (NGOs); and
- Foreign trusts and foundations.

To succeed in any fundraising activity, an organisation must do its homework. This means that the organisation must know who it will be approaching for funding. It is useful to have some background information on the funder and its way of working.

The organisation must know exactly what it wants to do with the funding. It must prepare a funding proposal for the donor that clearly states what it is planning, how much money it needs, how it will be managed, who will be involved and what the outcomes will be.

Finally, the organisation must realise that fundraising is not a once-off activity that ends when the funds are received. The manner in which a project is implemented, its success and the way in which this information is conveyed to the donor are also extremely important steps in the process. All of these steps have a direct impact on the current and future relationship between a donor and an organisation.

To a large extent, fundraising is a relationship-building activity. The stronger the relationship between an organisation and its potential donors, the better chance the organisation has of raising the necessary funds. The foundations of this relationship are mutual trust and respect. The best way for an organisation to gain the trust and respect of its donors is by acting professionally and honestly, and by achieving its stated goals.

2. Fundraising: The steps

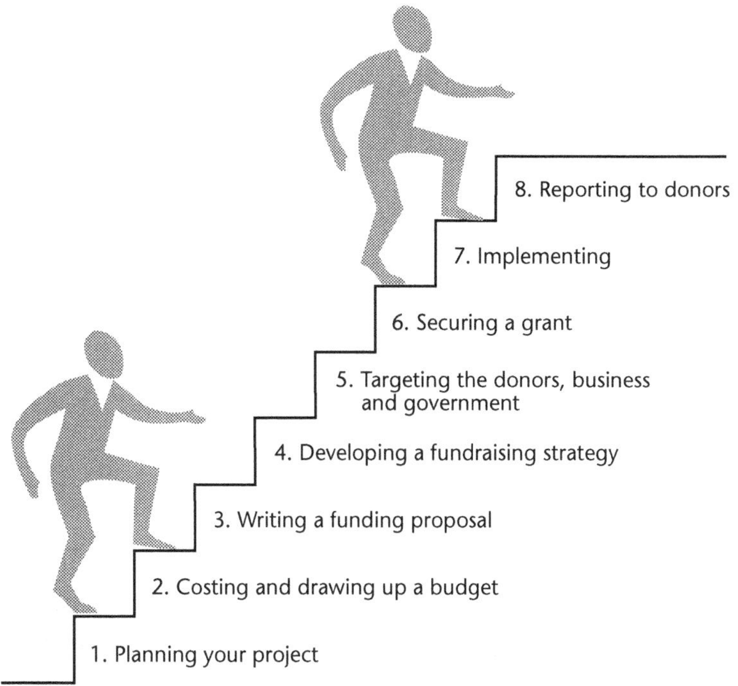

The Steps of Fundraising

From the picture above you can see that the fundraising process consists of eight separate steps. These steps represent the critical path that must be followed to ensure successful fundraising. As stated above, fundraising is not a once-off activity. For most organisations it is a continuous activity and therefore it is important that all of the steps in the picture are followed. In many cases, steps 7 and 8 are neglected because they come after the funding has been received. The danger in this is that the donor will hold it against you in the future. In other words, it is always important to remember that you may need a particular funder again in future and therefore you must treat them with as much respect and diginity as possible. In addition, it is also important to remember that funding is often tied to very strict rules and regulations regarding the implementation, monitoring and reporting of its use. This means that an organisation can actually get into trouble contractually if it does not implement, monitor or report in the method specified in the contract.

Although the fundraising process consists of eight separate steps, they are all inter-related and connnected with each other. Your fundraising will definitely not succeed if even one of these steps is neglected or forgotten.

The basic idea behind the eight steps is as follows:

Step 1: Planning your project

You have to be clear about exactly what it is that you need the money for. Donors do not give money unless you can clearly explain what it will be used for, how it will be used and who will be using it. There is absolutely no way that you will be able to raise significant funds without a very clearly thought out and detailed plan.

Step 2: Preparing a budget

Once you have clearly defined your project, you have to work out what it will cost to do the project. Once again, the funders will not fund a project unless you can provide them with a budget that shows exactly how much money will be needed and what that money will be needed for.

Step 3: Writing a funding proposal

Probably the most important of all the steps in the fundraising process is writing the funding proposal. This is the document that will be submitted to the different funders and it is the document they will use to decide whether or not to fund a specific project or organisation. The better the proposal, the better the chance that a project will be funded. The secret to proposal writing is in joining the project plan with the project budget in a way that makes sense to the people who read it.

Step 4: Developing a fundraising strategy

Once your proposal is completed, you have to work out a fundraising strategy. This means you have to decide how and where you are going to try to get the money for the proposal. As stated earlier, there are many ways to get funding. Unfortunately, not all of these can be used for every project. It is important to consider which would be the best way to raise funds for each specific proposal. It is also important to look at issues like which donors would be interested in a particular type of proposal, how much you are planning to get from each donor, whether you will approach multiple donors or whether you will try to get all the fundng from a single donor, etc.

Step 5: Targeting funders

One of the elements of step four is to identify the possible ways to raise funds. Step five takes this further by targeting the best possible funders identified in step four. You do this by learning as much as possible about the different prospective funders and using that information to identify the ones that are most likely to accept your proposal.

Step 6: Securing a grant

This step involves actually getting the money from the donors. It is often at this point that you will be informed of obligations and responsibilities tied to the funding.

Step 7: Implementation

Now that the funding is available you can begin to implement the plan. The important thing to remember is that there will definitely be responsibilities the funders expect from you. These could be to do with the way the project is implemented, the timelines or the reporting schedules. It is also important to remember that the money has been given for a specific project or purpose and cannot be used for something else without the approval of the donor.

Step 8: Reporting

The final step in the fundraising process is to report back to the funders. Some funders may want reporting on a regular basis throughout the project, others may want a report only once at the end of the project. The report usually has to explain what was done, what the results were and how the money was spent. The quality and detail of the report will probably play an important role in the donors' future decision on whether to fund your organisation or not. If the reporting is good the chance of future funding is good.

Each of the steps above will now be discussed in detail.

3. Project planning and development

The importance of project planning lies in the fact that this is the stage in the fundraising process in which you have to decide exactly what it is that you require funding for. Unfortunately, donors aren't usually willing to give money that can be spent in a discretionary fashion. They will only give money if they know exactly what those funds are going to be used for. In order to give them this information you have to carefully plan and develop a project and present it to them. In general, project planning and development involves the following six steps:

Step 1: Determining the need for the project
The organisation must look at the reasons for the specific organisation or project. There are many ways to do this, but the most important element is to find out why a specific project is needed in a specific community, region or country.

Step 2: Situation and problem analysis
Once you have identified a need for a project in step one, you have to go further by looking closely at the need; you need to find out exactly what the current situation and problems are, why they have arisen and how they can be addressed. An example would be an HIV/AIDS project. In most parts of our country HIV/AIDS is an enormous problem, but the exact nature of that problem may vary from town to town. In some towns prevention is an issue that needs to be addressed, while in other towns there is a more urgent need to address the problem of AIDS orphans. Simply identifying HIV/AIDS as a problem that needs to be addressed is not enough. You must go further to identify what exactly the problem is about HIV/AIDS in the community that you want to serve.

Step 3: Choice of suitable project (prioritising needs)
Once you have identified the exact nature of the problem you want to address, you have to decide how you can best do this. You may come up with several possible projects. Unfortunately, you will not be able to do all of them and therefore you must decide which one is the best for you. In the HIV/AIDS example it is possible that you have identified the problems of prevention, education and

orphans, but your organisation is better suited to dealing with education. Therefore you will choose a project concept that has to do with education rather than projects that address prevention or orphans.

Step 4: Project formulation and planning

At this stage you should be clear about what project you want to attempt. Your next step is to begin the process of clearly defining exactly what it is that you will be doing, with whom, where you will be doing it and over what period of time. Specific issues that also need to be addressed are the objectives, goals and outcomes of the project; the beneficiaries of the project; and the stakeholders. It is important for both you and any future funders that this is very clearly spelt out. A funder will very quickly pick up if you are not certain about what you want to do. You will also need this information to accurately design the project.

Step 5: Project design

This is the point at which you combine all the information you collected in the previous steps into a coherent project plan. It covers everything from providing exact timelines for the project to explaining the methodology that will be used to achieve the project goals. It is also at this point that you will determine the different resources required to implement the project.

Step 6: Choosing the project team

The final step in this process involves selecting the project team. You will have to decide who in the organisation and/or its partners will be actively involved in the project and you will have to specify what each of these people or organisations will be doing. This is important for planning and budgeting purposes. It is important for planning because you need to make sure that the relevant people are available and willing to assist and it is important for budgeting because you have to make sure that the budget provides sufficient funds for the different people.

4. Budgeting

The budget is an organisation's most important financial planning tool. It emerges directly from the objectives or outputs of the organisation and shows exactly what the organisation expects its activities during a specific time period to cost. In other words, the budget is based on the actual amount of money that an organisation expects to get and that it knows it will have to spend. It is not only a strategy to help manage income or cut expenses. It shows the actual situation for a given time period. The budgeting process involves the following steps:

Step 1: The first step in any budgeting process is to make sure that the person or people doing the budget know exactly what the activity or activities are that are being budgeted for. This can only be done if you have clearly planned all of the activities for the budget period.

Step 2: Once you know what will be done, you have to find out all the possible areas of expenditure. These are called the expenditure line items in your budget. Each different expense is a different line item. An example could be a line item for transport and a line item for salaries. It is extremely important that every single expense is reflected in the budget as a line item.

Step 3: Once the different (expenditure) items have been identified, it is also necessary to identify the different income items. This is exactly the same as the expenditure items except in this case you are listing all of the sources of income.

Step 4: The next step involves working out exactly how much money will be needed for each expenditure item and how much money will be received from each income item. These figures must be as accurate as possible because they often cannot be changed once the project has begun. They will show if there is enough money coming in to cover the amount of money that will be going out. If there is not enough, the expenses must be reduced or extra income must be found.

Step 5: Once you have finalised your income and expenditure budgets, it is important to work out a cash flow budget based on those figures. The cash flow budget not only shows how much money will come in and go out, it also adds a time element. In other words it shows when the money will come in or go out. This is important because you have to make sure that your income and expenses are co-ordinated. For instance, you cannot start spending money if you have not yet received any.

4.1 Budgeting checklist

Step 1: Plan your activities for the period in question

↓

Step 2: Work out what your different expenditure items will be

↓

Step 3: Work out what your different income items will be

↓

Step 4: Find out exactly what each of your expenditure items will cost

↓

Step 5: Work out exactly what your income will be

↓

Step 6: Work out if there is any shortfall between income and expenditure

↓

Step 7: From your income and expenditure budget work out a cash flow budget

↓

Step 8: Present your draft budgets for comments

↓

Step 9: Change your budgets if necessary

↓

Step 10: Finalise your income and expenditure budgets and your cash flow budget.

Example: Project budget

Income		
Donations	500 000	
Internal income	50 000	
Interest	20 000	
Total income		**570 000**
Expenditure		
Salaries	350 000	
Printing and stationery	100 000	
Telephone and fax	50 000	
Rent	50 000	
Venue hire	30 000	
Total expenditure		**580 000**
Excess/(deficit)		**(10 000)**

5. Writing a funding proposal

The general purpose of any proposal is to persuade the readers to do something. This can be achieved by answering questions about WHAT you are proposing, HOW you plan to do it, WHEN you plan to do it and HOW MUCH it is going to cost.

For this reason, writing a funding proposal is possibly the most important step in the fundraising process. It is at this point that you must put together all the information and work you did in the previous steps to create a document that can be presented to potential funders. Their decision to fund the project will be based upon it.

If the proposal is not good or is not acceptable to the funders there is almost no chance that they will provide funding. Therefore it is extremely important that you make sure that the proposal is well-written, clearly states what you want to do and how you plan to do it, and provides exact details of the amount of money that will be needed. One mistake can ruin the entire proposal and cost you the chance of getting money from a donor.

In general, proposal writing is a skill that anyone can learn but it does require a lot of practice and a lot of attention to detail. There are several general rules that should be followed to ensure that you produce the best possible proposal. They include:

- **Do your homework:** This means that you must not only complete all the steps in the project-planning process, you must also go out of your way to learn as much as possible about the prospective funder/s you want to approach. In most cases donors have their own formats or requirements for proposals and it is important for the proposal writer to use and understand these guidelines. A well-written proposal will mean nothing if it does not meet the requirements of a specific donor.
- **Follow instructions:** In most cases donors have specific forms and instructions that have to be used and followed when you approach them for funding, for example, the need to submit applications or proposals before a certain date. It is the proposal writer's responsibility to ensure that the proposal is prepared in time to meet these deadlines. Proposals that are submitted late will not be considered.
- **Be patient:** Proposal writing can be a very long and difficult process, but it is a process that must be followed. If you take a shortcut or if you do not complete all of the steps in the planning process there is a good chance that you will not be successful.
- **Stay focused:** When writing your proposal you must do your best to stay focused on the message you are trying to convey. Not only must you explain the project, you must also provide proof and background information for any problem statements that you

make. Your proposed project should be logical, clearly outlined, justified and budgeted.

- **Make it look good:** It is very important that your proposal looks professional. That means you must make sure that is neat, well organised and does not contain spelling and/or grammatical errors. The proposal represents you and your organisation. If it looks good you look good; if it looks bad you look bad.
- **Ask for help:** If you have any uncertainties about your proposal, don't be afraid to ask for assistance. In general it is also a very good idea to ask someone else to read your proposal after you have finished writing it. They can help identify spelling and grammatical errors and give you an honest opinion on whether the proposal is clear and understandable.
- **Learn from rejection:** Unfortunately most of your proposals will be rejected for one reason or another. This does, however, provide a good opportunity to improve your proposal-writing skills. If at all possible you should use these rejections to review your proposals and to identify possible weaknesses. As your proposals improve, so will your success rate.

5.1 The elements of a proposal

The basic structure of a proposal, as with any other document, is simple; it must have a beginning (the introduction), a middle (the body of the proposal) and an end (the conclusion/recommendation). The introduction presents and summarises the problem you intend to solve and your solution to that problem. The body of the proposal explains the details of the solution, including how the job will be done, what method will be used to do it, when the work will be done and what the expected costs are. The conclusion should emphasise the benefits that will be gained from your solution to the problem and should urge the reader to take action.

These three features of the proposal need to be reflected in the format. The precise format will usually be prescribed by the donors and it is extremely important that you always follow the exact specifications of the donors in the applications. Nevertheless, in most cases proposals will contain the following elements:

5.1.1 The cover page

- The first thing to consider in preparing your cover page is whether the specific donor has any specifications for the cover sheet. If so, these must be strictly adhered to.
- In general, the cover page should include the name and address of your organisation, the title of the proposed project, the signatures of the relevant manager/s in the organisation and a reference to any partner organisations.
- Make sure your title is clear and unambiguous. The title should paint a clear picture of what you want to do.
- Try to keep your title short and sweet.
- Make sure your cover page is neat and professional. This is the first impression on the donor so make sure it is a good one.

5.1.2 Executive summary

- The purpose of the executive summary is to provide a short introduction to the project. It should include brief information on the aims and objectives, the resources required and the expected outcomes.

- The most important thing to remember about the executive summary is that it must be short and concise, but at the same time it must paint a clear picture of the proposal for the reader. It is not necessary to include details that will be explained later in the proposal.
- It is useful if you include in the executive summary why a specific proposal would meet the objectives of the donor. This shows that you have done your homework about the funder and should encourage the funder to read further.
- If you are working with partner organisations it is important that they and their role are also mentioned in the executive summary.
- The best time to prepare the executive summary is after you have completed the rest of the proposal. At that point you will have a clear idea of what is important and what needs to be highlighted.

5.1.3 Organisational details

- The purpose of this section is to provide the donor with a brief introduction to the organisation or organisations that will be implementing the project.
- This should include items such as the structure and management of the organisation, its mission and vision, the history of the organisation and the reason it was formed.

5.1.4 Needs assessment

- This section provides a detailed analysis of the problem or need that you are hoping to address.
- It should include a description of the specific population or community that you are intending to

assist as well as a clear definition of the specific need or problem that will be addressed.

- All of your assertions regarding the problem or need must be supported by independent, objective and qualified third-party research.
- It might also be necessary at this stage to differentiate your project from other similar projects. This can be done by showing how you will extend work that has already been done, or by showing how you will avoid the mistakes that were made in previous similar projects, or by showing how your project has a unique approach that has not been tried before.
- If possible, at this point you should try to show why your organisation is particularly well placed to implement the project. This could include reasons such as geographic proximity, previous experience or existing relationships with the target population.
- In this section of your proposal you also need to explain whether the problem or need, as well as the solution, are long- or short-term. This is important because it will support other elements of your proposal that relate to methodology, timeframe and budgets.

5.1.5 Programme goals and objectives

- In this section you must clearly explain what the expected outcomes of the project will be. This is achieved by describing the specific goals that you have set for yourself, as well as the specific objectives through which you will achieve these goals. Your goals are the statements of what you want to accomplish. Your objectives are the specific things that you will do to achieve the goals.

- As far as possible you should try to develop objectives that can be measured. An example would be to train a specific number of people. At the end of the project your objective can be measured according to whether or not you were able to train the number of people you specified. From the example below you can see that the goal is a broad statement, while the objectives are specific activities that need to be undertaken to achieve the goal. The number of goals and objectives will vary greatly from one project to another.

Example: Goals and objectives

Goal	Objectives
Create community awareness about HIV/AIDS.	✧ Host two community forum meetings; ✧ Arrange four HIV/AIDS training sessions; ✧ Print and distribute information brochures to the entire community (+/- 10 000 people).

5.1.6 Methodology

- The first thing you must do in this section is explain in detail what methods you will be using.
- Secondly, you must make sure that your methods are directly and clearly tied to your objectives. In other words, you must explain how your methods will help you to achieve your objectives.
- In cases where other organisations have used different methods to address a similar problem, it might be necessary to explain why your specific methods will be more successful.

5.1.7 Activity plan

- The activity plan combines your objectives and methodologies into a breakdown of exactly what will be done during the different phases of the project.

- This includes every single activity from the planning phase to the evaluation phase at the end of the project.
- The activity plan uses the methodology that has been chosen and turns that methodology into very specific actions or activities. These activities are then carried out to achieve the objectives that have been identified. From the example below you will note that the activity plan is simply an extension of the goals and objectives. The activity plan adds the exact activities or tasks that need to be performed to achieve each of the different objectives.

Example: Activity plan

Goal	Objectives	Activities
Create community awareness about HIV/AIDS.	✧ Host two community forum meetings.	✧ Set date for community meetings; ✧ Invite participants; ✧ Book venues; ✧ Arrange refreshments; ✧ Invite guest speakers.

5.1.8 Timeframe

- In this section you provide details of the timeframe over which your proposed project will run. This means the date you propose to begin and the date you expect to finish.
- In addition to providing the overall timeframe, you may also be required to add your timeframe to your activity plan. By doing this you not only provide information on what you will be doing, you also provide details about when each activity will take place and how long each activity will take. Using the

activity plan above, you would add an additional column on the right to indicate when each activity must be performed or how long each activity will take.

Example: Activity plan + timeframes

Goal	Objectives	Activities	Timeframe
Create community awareness about HIV/AIDS.	✧ Host two community forum meetings.	✧ Set date for community meetings;	01/12/05
		✧ Invite participants;	05/12/05
		✧ Book venues;	01/12/05
		✧ Arrange refreshment;	07/12/05
		✧ Invite guest speakers.	05/12/05

5.1.9 Project resources (personnel/facilities/equipment/supplies, etc)

- This section must be used to explain what resources will be required for the project and to give reasons for each resource.
- You must also explain what resources you already have and which you still need to get.
- You must explain who will be involved in the project and why.
- You also need to say how many of the personnel on the project will have to be paid out of the project budget and why.
- You need to explain whether you will need to acquire or rent any facilities or equipment and you will have to explain what they will be used for.
- If you have access to facilities and equipment, include this in the proposal because it shows that your organisation is contributing something to the project.
- If you have to purchase equipment for the project, it is important that you list everything that you will

need. If possible, you should also provide actual quotes for the equipment. A very strong motivation and justification for the equipment will also be needed because funders generally do not like giving money to purchase equipment.

5.1.10 Budget/funding requirements

- By this point in the fundraising process you should already have prepared a budget, which must be included in the proposal. (See pages 9-12.)
- It is very important that your budget is realistic. Do not over-inflate it.
- Check that your budget contains all of the items that the specific funder wants.
- You also need to indicate whether you will require the entire grant at once or whether it can be paid in phases. Many funders prefer to pay in phases because it gives them control over the project and the money.

5.1.11 Monitoring and evaluation plan

- This section describes the plan that you have developed for ensuring that the project meets the goals and objectives that have been set.
- This plan should include information on who will be doing the evaluation, what exactly will be measured and monitored, what instruments, criteria or data will be used to do the monitoring and what methodology will be followed.
- This plan does not have to be too elaborate, but it is important to show to donors that you have not forgotten about it.
- Your evaluation plan must be directly linked to the achievement of the project objectives. A simple

evaluation plan is based on your activity plan with an additional column specifying what progress has been made on each activity and objective.
- If possible, your evaluation plan should include a section on the impact and sustainability of the outcomes after the project has ended. This could leave the door open for follow-up projects in the future.

5.1.12 Annexures

- The annexures are usually secondary documents that support the proposal.
- Often the annexures that are used are specifically required by the donor or donors. In these cases it is important to ensure that all of the relevant documents are attached.
- They could include the organisation's financial statements, letters of support, curriculum vitae of the personnel involved, background information on the organisation, etc.

6. Developing a fundraising strategy

6.1 Understanding your environment/environmental scanning

The successful development of a fundraising strategy, like all other strategies, depends on the availability of information. In short, it is impossible to plan unless you have adequate information. The information that you need can be divided into several categories. These include:

- understanding your organisation and its goals and objectives;
- understanding what you need and how much you need;

- understanding the external environment within which you will be working; and
- understanding your competitors (other organisations who are also looking for funding).

You need information on all of these aspects before you can even begin to develop a strategy. A strategy that is based on incorrect information or assumptions is doomed to fail right from the start. Each of these categories will be discussed in more detail:

- **Internal: Understanding your organisation and its goals and objectives:** The starting point for developing any strategy must always be your organisation itself. It is very important that all the people involved in developing the strategy clearly understand the overall goals of the organisation and the specific goals of the project or programme, and how they fit into the organisational goals. In addition, everyone must understand how the organisation intends to achieve its goals and why the organisation wants to achieve these goals. This information should then be combined with an honest analysis of the resources of the organisation to identify the *strengths and weaknesses* of the organisation to guide the strategy that is adopted.

  The answers to these questions will have a direct impact on the type of fundraising strategies that an organisation can adopt. If, for example, an organisation has a severe staff shortage it would not make sense to develop a strategy that relies on a labour-intensive activity. Also, if an organisation's goals or ideals differ drastically from those of a prospective funder it would not make sense to waste time or damage your organisation's reputation or image by approaching such a funder. By forming a clear image of your own organisation you will avoid many pitfalls and you will ensure that all of your fundraising activities are aligned with the goals of the organisation.

It is usually assumed that everyone in an organisation shares an understanding of its goals and objectives as well as its strengths and weaknesses. Unfortunately, that is not usually the case. For this reason it is important that this exercise be the first step in every strategy development process.

- **Internal: Understand your needs:** Once you have a good understanding of your organisation as a whole, it is important to develop a clear understanding of the specific needs that you are trying to address through the fundraising process. In other words, you have to decide what you are trying to raise money for and how much you need.

  For the most part, this question should already have been answered during your project planning and budgeting steps. If you reach this stage and you are still not sure what the money will be used for and how much you will need, then you urgently need to go back to steps one and two in the fundraising process. As stated earlier, it is incredibly important to *do your homework*. The entire fundraising process can fail if you skip a single step in the process.
- **External: Political-economic-sociological-technological (PEST) analysis and opportunities and threats analysis:** This is an important and often overlooked part of developing any strategy. Planning or strategising does not happen in a

vacuum; there are many external factors that can influence a plan or strategy and that, therefore, have to be considered. For example, there are some countries that do not allow foreign donors to fund local organisations and an organisation that is unaware of this and that receives foreign funding could face severe penalties.

There are two tools that an organisation can use to ensure that it has a good understanding of the external environment, namely a PEST analysis and an opportunities and threats analysis. At first they look quite intimidating, but in reality they are quite simple to use. The PEST analysis is designed to give a good general overview of the environment by looking at four categories. These categories are:

- **P** – Political and legal environment
  It is important to understand the political and legal environment at local, provincial and national levels and how that environment will have an impact on your organisation. You need to consider things like whether or not the government supports or opposes what you are doing and whether there are any legal restrictions on what you are doing. Another important element to investigate is the tax legislation and how that can influence your fundraising activities.

- **E** – Economic environment
  Once again, you must look at the economy at local, provincial and national levels. Since you are looking for funding, it is important to find out whether the economy is strong enough to support

local funders or whether you should rather look for international funding. In addition, it is important to consider the impact of the economy on the long-term sustainability of your organisation and/or projects. This means that you must consider things like inflation when you are working on budgets if you are asking for long-term funding. Otherwise over time you will find that your funds run out. If the inflation rate is stable this is easy, but in many cases inflation is very unstable and that makes planning very difficult.

- **S** – Socio-cultural environment
  You must consider things like the structure, lifestyles, cultures, religions, languages, attitudes and needs of the community/ies you want to help, as well as those of the people or organisations that you may want to approach for funding. It may be that the community you are planning to help has a objection to receiving assistance from a specific funder or country, or prospective funders might have social or cultural objections to funding certain types of projects. By knowing this in advance, you will be able to save time and effort and ensure that you don't approach the wrong funders or use the wrong fundraising method.

- **T** – Technological environment
  The technological environment refers to things like the availability of technology within the organisation and the availability of skilled people to operate it. In addition, you need to look at

ways to use the available skills and technology to achieve the organisation's goals. The best example is the use of the internet as a fundraising tool. It makes no sense developing an on-line fundraising strategy if your organisation does not have the necessary skills or technology or if the technology is not available to the people you are going to approach for funds.

Once you have completed the PEST exercise, you can use this information to do a threat or opportunity analysis. Basically, this means that you use the information about your environment to identify threats to your organisation and opportunities for your organisation. A threat would be something like legislation that prohibits certain types of fundraising, while an opportunity could be something like the availability of government funds for the type of project you would like to do. Once you have identified the major threats or opportunities (usually not more than five of each), you can use this information to develop strategies that will minimise the threats and maximise the opportunities.

- **External: Understanding your competitors:** The unfortunate fact of the matter is that there is tremendous competition for donor funding. For this reason it is important to know who your possible competitors might be and how you can differentiate yourself from them. If you cannot differentiate your organisation from other organisations, then you need to ask yourself whether you actually need to exist at all.

Differentiation can be based on a million different factors, from where you are located to the way in which you do your work. The importance from a fundraising point of view is that your organisation must be able to show prospective funders what makes you different from all the other organisations requesting funding. This obviously becomes very difficult if you don't know anything about the other organisations, especially those that do similar work to yours.

A final point to remember is that this is not simply about competition. It is very possible that there is a need for a number of different organisations doing similar work. They need to be differentiated though to ensure that everyone is not doing exactly the same work in exactly the same place. HIV/AIDS, for instance, involves many organisations in many different areas of work, which requires a huge amount of funding. If everyone simply stated that they were dealing with HIV/AIDS they would probably not all be funded, but if each organisation specified the type of work they are doing or in which locations they are working, many more organisations will get funding.

6.2 Strategy formulation

At this point you should have a clear understanding of your specific needs, your strengths and weaknesses and the environment in which you are working and this information can now be used to develop a fundraising strategy or action plan. This can be achieved by using the information gathered during the above process to answer the following simple questions.

- **Who?** This refers to who should be approached for funding as well as whom within the organisation should be involved in the fundraising process. In terms of funders, it is also important to decide at this stage whether you will approach one funder only or many funders.

- **What?** This refers to what type of fundraising activities should be used. Should all the funds come from local and international donors or should the organisation arrange activities to raise its own funds. There are thousands of different ways to raise funds and it is up to each organisation to use the information at its disposal to decide which methods are best suited to their circumstances and needs.
- **Where?** Organisations must decide in which geographic location, as well as at what level, they will be doing their fundraising. A good example would be to decide whether or not to limit your fundraising to local government departments or whether to approach provincial government departments as well.
- **When?** This question will be answered in two ways. Firstly, the organisation will have to determine what its needs are. In other words, how urgently do they need the money? Secondly, the organisation will have to use the information that it has on the donor environment to see when donors prefer to be approached for funds. Many donor organisations have strict deadlines for the submission of project proposals and it is therefore important for organisations to take this into account. They also have to consider matters like holiday seasons and the availability of people when they are planning fundraising activities. Planning an activity when most of the community is away on holiday does not make sense.

- **How much?** This relates to both the total amount of money that is needed as well as the way in which different fundraising activities will be used to raise that amount. If an organisation is extremely lucky, it will get all of its funding from one donor or activity. However this usually does not happen and the organisation has to plan several activities or approach several donors to reach its target amount. For this reason it is important to specify all of the proposed activities as well as the amounts that the organisation expects to raise through each.

The final step in the strategy process is to capture the answers to all of these questions in a strategy/activity document. There are many different ways to do this, but the simplest way is to use an activity plan, discussed earlier. Your goal is simple; you want to raise a specific amount of money. Your objectives are the different activities that you will undertake to try to raise the money. It is useful to include the specific amounts that you hope to raise through each activity. Your activities are those specific actions that you need to undertake to make the activities happen. Finally your timeframes refer to the total amount of time you will need as well as the specific time periods that are allocated to each of the activities. Although not always necessary, it is also possible to add an additional column to your activity plan that specifies who will be responsible for each activity.

Example: Strategic/activity plan

Goal	Objective	Activities	Timeframe	Responsibility
Raise R500 000 for HIV/AIDS education in the Northern Province.	✧ Raise R400 000 through donations from international donors.	✧ Identify international donors;	01/12/05	Name of the specific individual, unit or section responsible.
		✧ Get contact details of international donors;	05/12/05	
		✧ Prepare project proposals;	31/12/05	
		✧ Submit project proposals	15/01/06	

Model for strategy development

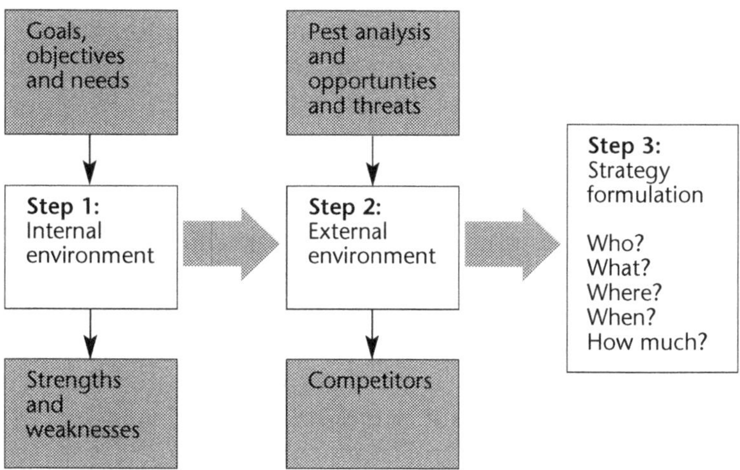

7. Targeting donors

The purpose of targeting is to ensure that you approach the correct donors with your proposal. There are thousands of potential donors all over the world and it is virtually impossible to approach all of them for every project you plan. The fundamental problem is that not all donors are necessarily interested in the specific work your organisation wants to do. As discussed above, it is possible that there are political or cultural differences between you and certain donors that prevent you from approaching them. By targeting specific donors with whom you think you have a good chance of success you are able to save a lot of time, money and effort.

Targeting is basically a two-step process. Firstly, you need to use the information that you gathered during your strategy planning session to identify all of the possible sources of funding for your project and/or organisation. In practical terms this means that you must compile a list of every possible source of funding that you can think of. This could include local donors, international donors, individuals or organisations. As your organisation grows you should always try to keep an up to date list of possible donors, which will make this exercise easier.

Secondly, once your list has been completed, you must scrutinise each donor on the list to identify those that are the best match for your organisation or the specific project that you are planning to launch. The specific criteria you use will differ from project to project, but in all cases they will be based on the information that you gathered during your environmental scanning (PEST and threat and opportunity analyses). If your environmental scanning was done properly, you should have a very good idea of which donors you can and cannot approach.

8. Securing the funding

This is not only the moment the donor agrees to fund all or part of your organisation or project; it is also the moment in which the donor informs you of the terms and conditions under which they will provide the funding.

Donations and grants come in many forms and not all of these forms are helpful to an organisation. In general, the ideal situation is to get a long-term organisational grant that can be used flexibly to achieve the overall goals of the organisation. Unfortunately, it is becoming more and more difficult to obtain these types of grants. In most cases, donors prefer to provide funding on a project-by-project basis.

When dealing with donors at this stage of the process, it is important to realise that you may not get exactly what you want. As a result, it is important to evaluate each grant on a case-by-case basis. Even if you don't get everything that you want, you should at least strive to get a grant or funding package that suits your organisation and will work best for you. In most cases, it is possible to negotiate a grant/funding agreement that will be acceptable to both your organisation and the donor. If this is not possible, you have to decide whether your organisation is willing or able to work under the terms and conditions imposed by the funder. In a few exceptional cases it may not be possible and you may even have to decline the money. If you do agree to accept the funding, the terms and conditions will be formalised in a funding agreement that is a legally binding document between you and the donor.

A final aspect to remember at this stage is the importance of clarifying how and when the funding will be made available. In some cases, donors prefer to reimburse organisations for expenses incurred, whilst in other case they will pay a grant up front and expect the organisation to provide them with a financial report at the end of the project. This is an extremely important issue to consider because it could have a severe impact on the cash flow of the organisation. It is meaningless to accept reimbursement funding if your organisation does not have sufficient funds to pay the up-front expenses or if the up-front expenses will place an unnecessary burden on the organisation's cash flow.

9. Implementing the project

The implementation and reporting steps in the fundraising process are often overlooked because they usually occur after the funding has been received and therefore aren't really considered part of the process. The problem with this approach is that it looks at fundraising as a once-off event, instead of an ongoing process that continues as long as your organisation exists.

The successful implementation of a project is possibly the single most important marketing tool that any CBO possesses. Not only does it create a positive image of the organisation with the existing funder, it also provides concrete evidence of the organisation's abilities and professionalism that can be presented to other prospective donors. At the same time, an unsuccessful project creates negative impressions with existing and potential donors.

Much of the success of the fundraising process depends on existing relationships between organisations and their donors. It is usually much easier for existing organisations with successful track records to get funding than it is for new organisations. The best way to maintain and strengthen these relationships is through the successful implementation of projects and the proper use of donor funds.

10. Reporting to donors

Donors expect to be informed of what is going on in the organisation or the specific project; this is the final step in the fundraising process. In almost all cases it is an obligation that is specified in the funding agreement and in most cases there are very specific criteria for the content, format and timing of reports.

Not only do these reports keep the donor informed of the progress of a project, they also provide the donor with justification to continue with a project. It is important to remember that fundraising does not stop once the money has been received. If the funders do not think that the money is being wisely spent or that the project is achieving its stated objectives, they have the right to stop further funding or to request a refund of earlier funding. To prevent this, organisations must ensure that they strictly comply with all of the relevant reporting criteria.

In general, donor reports consist of two elements, a narrative report and a financial report. The narrative section is a progress report on the implementation of the project. This includes what has been done, what has been achieved, what problems have been experienced and what still needs to be done. The financial report is a summary of the financial situation of the project. For the most part, this will compare the actual money received and spent with the amounts that were specified in the project budget, as well as the amounts that must still be spent. In this way the donor can continuously monitor the use of the money that was granted and ensure that it is spent in a way that achieves the goals of the project.

As stated earlier, each grant/funding agreement will have its own stipulations about when and how reports need to be submitted, but all donors require at least that a final project report be submitted at the end of the project. This report summarises the implementation and finances of the entire project. The actual format for these reports may also be specified in the funding agreement, but generally the following sections need to be included:

- **Title:** This should include the name of the project, the name of the organisation and any reference numbers that the funder might give you.
- **Time span:** This specifies the time period that you are reporting on and states whether the report is an interim report or a final report.
- **Original objectives:** This section highlights what the project was designed to achieve.
- **Achievements:** This explains what was done and what was achieved in relation to the original objectives that were set. In other words it should show how much progress was made in achieving the project objectives.
- **Financial report:** This should compare the actual financial situation to the original project budget. It is also useful to explain any surpluses or deficits.
- **Future plans:** If the report is an interim report, this section will be used to describe further implementation. If the report is final, this section can be used to show how the results of the project will be used in future and it may even be used to enquire about additional or new funding to extend or build on the completed project.

STRATEGIC PLANNING

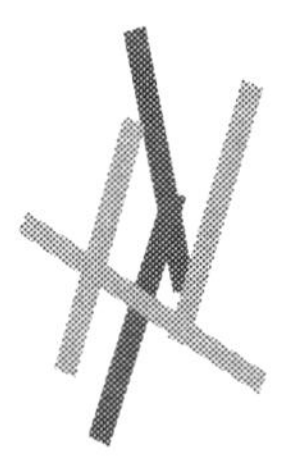

1. Introduction

All organisations face a world that is rapidly changing. These changes are taking place largely because of technology, which leads to faster contact between people, economic markets, different governments and large corporations.

This increasing pace brings benefits, but it also brings disadvantages.

Globalisation – as it is called – affects all organisations, including community-based organisations (CBOs), the world over. It is important that the power of a changing world is harnessed to the advantage of people in local communities.

For example, you might belong to a CBO that focuses on women's issues and one of the key projects is a sewing project, which sells its products in a big city. Fashion trends change all the time; you have to keep up with the changes otherwise your products might be discarded or sent back to you. You might make skirts using blue material and they are not bought because the fashion houses in Paris have decided that purple is *the* colour that month.

In the ever-increasing pace of the world it is important that you include strategic planning to ensure your survival and growth. This notebook will help you to understand what strategic planning is, how to plan strategically and how to ensure that strategic planning is implemented in your organisation.

2. What is strategic planning?

Strategic planning is a process an organisation follows that is disciplined and thorough. It will take note of the internal dynamics of the organisation, as well as the external dynamics of the world outside the organisation.

It will analyse whether the organisation is effective in its goals and objectives. It will establish whether the organisation needs to change its direction to fulfil its purpose. In other words it is a management tool that will help an organisation to do a better job.

The reason that the process is strategic is that critical choices will need to be made. If the understanding of the organisation's objectives is clear, there needs to be an awareness of the resources the organisation has available to spend on the objectives. Strategic planning helps you to respond to the external environment in the most effective way.

Strategic planning is not an activity that is 'once-off'. It is something that takes place over time. It requires the organisational resources and the thinking caps of as many people as possible.

It is not – as most people think – a process that is conducted at a one- or two-day planning session. It is a process that is planned in advance, involves different levels of decision-making and will result in a plan of action that needs to be monitored as it is implemented. The plan could change as circumstances change.

? WHAT ?

WHY ?

? HOW ?

WHO

However, at its most simple, strategic planning is what to do, why it should be done, how it should be done and who should do it.

It is important to remember that there is a difference between doing everything you would like to do and doing only what you can do given the resources and the context. This is strategic planning. When you make decisions about what you can or cannot do as an organisation, you are choosing a strategy.

Strategic planning is not a tool that will be unfamiliar to you. After all, when you make decisions at the beginning of every year about how you spend your household budget, you are making strategic decisions. The key difference is the discipline process that is followed when organisations make strategic decisions. The methods used in strategic planning have been around for many years.

3. Why should you do strategic planning?

The simplest reason for your organisation to do strategic planning is to give you an edge. There might be two or three organisations that have the same objectives, the same resources and the same skills. You can be sure that the organisation that has put effort into planning its future and into the effective management of its resources will do a better job than the organisation that has not.

It is important also to remember that often people begin to think about planning only when they have problems. Strategic planning helps your organisation to avoid crises now and in the future. If you plan and think ahead, you will get more resources; you will have more skills; you will be better able to to serve the community in which you are based.

By encouraging others in your organisation to plan strategically, you will get fresh ideas from different places and people. Others members of the organisation – not just the leadership – will be more committed. This will enable you to deliver services of a higher quality to the members of your community.

If done properly, strategic planning can help you to identify the causes of some of the problems in your organisation and it will enable you to come up with solutions.

4. Where does strategic planning come from?

Strategic planning originated in military operations. In times of war it was necessary to understand your own military strength and to be aware of the strength of the enemy. High-level planning took place, usually by the generals, and then the different levels of the army executed the plans.

Of course, if the enemy was more strategic in its planning than you were, then you would suffer setbacks. You would have to go back to the drawing board because the enemy could surprise you by using new technology or a different strategic approach.

Planning in a military environment is hierarchical and there are many 'secrets' that are not shared with the larger organisation. A foot soldier might not know why he is being instructed to go to a particular area, however he would be expected to follow orders. The primary reason for generals to plan was so that they would have a competitive advantage over the enemy.

In the 1950s the business world began to use military-like strategic planning methods to give themselves a strategic advantage over their competitors. In many ways the methods used by business managers were similar to those used by the military. In those days usually it was only the top level in the organisation that took part in the process. The rest of the organisation, or the workers, would follow orders from higher up the ladder.

However, over time it became noticeable that new and interesting ideas could be found among the workers, who worked more closely to the manufacturing process and knew what problems might arise. These days more people are included in the strategic planning process of a business environment.

In the past 20 years the non-profit sector has begun to use strategic planning as one of its organisational management tools. The reason for this was that as more organisations were established, the competition for funding, for skilled people and for delivering services became more intense.

The number of CBOs has mushroomed and although different organisations have similar objectives, one CBO might have more resources than another.

It follows then that regular strategic planning will give your CBO a competitive advantage over other organisations.

5. Benefits of strategic planning

It is important to remember that to benefit, you must be committed and complete the strategic planning process effectively. If you follow the processes outlined in this notebook, you should find that your successful strategic planning process will:

- Lead to effective action;
- Build a shared vision based on common values;
- Be focused and sensitive to the environment in which the organisation operates;
- Be based on good information; and
- Allow all participants to be open and to challenge the status quo (current way of operating).

If you have conducted a successful strategic planning process, benefits to your organisation will:

- Result in a participatory and inclusive process, which will lead to the board and the staff or volunteers taking ownership;
- Help you to define the purpose of your organisation clearly, which will lead to realistic planning;

Your organisation will be able to go from strength to strength...

- Help you to realise what activities will help you to achieve your overall goals so that you do not waste time on activities that hinder progress; and
- Help organisations to be accountable to communities by effectively communicating with the people they serve and listening to the community to improve their service.

As with all other tools, the more you plan strategically, the better you will become at it. Strategic planning can help your organisation grow and become more effective in your community.

6. Who should be included in the strategic planning process?

Your first task is to set up a planning committee that should include:

- A decision-maker from the board;
- A senior decision-maker in the organisation;
- Someone who is good at facilitation;
- Staff or volunteers; and
- Someone who represents the community that you serve.

The planning committee should ensure that during the process of strategic planning it involves the following roleplayers:

- Board members – at least the chairperson;
- Leadership of the organisation – the director and other managers;
- Staff and/or volunteers;
- Members of the organisation;
- Representatives of the community you serve; and
- External stakeholders (either people who are

knowledgeable in your field or people who might have an effect on or influence your work, such as a local councillor).

It is important for the planning committee to find the best way to involve each of the roleplayers. Some might need to be consulted only once. Some might be involved in many aspects of the planning, while others might give you advice or input on a particular matter.

People outside your organisation might be able to help because they think differently. We are all informed by our own subjective view of the world and the work we do. It is helpful to have people from outside the organisation to help you discover what the perception of the organisation is in the community. They can tell you what local government thinks about the work you do.

People on the outside can give you insight into what donors think about your organisation. There are many other topics outside people can help you with; it is up to you to establish who would be most useful and how they could help.

You should make every effort to establish who the people are who could help you to plan strategically. If you do not, you may leave out vital information.

Once you have your planning committee in place and you are aware of all the people you should include in the process, you are ready to begin.

7. What are the steps in the strategic planning process?

Each of these steps will be dealt with in detail. To begin the strategic planning process you should have a broad overview of what it is that you are embarking on. The following six steps make up the strategic planning process:

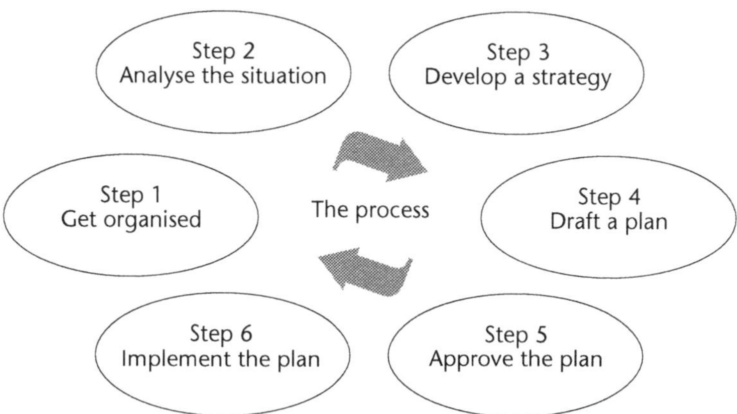

7. 1. Getting organised

It is important to get support from all the different sections of your organisation before you begin planning. If you don't do this, you might encounter resistance when you put together the strategic planning process. You need the support of the board and the senior leadership of the organisation.

You need to decide what kind of planning process you will use. Some examples of the choices you will need to make are:

- Will you have a one- or two-day session?
- Will you invite everyone or just certain people in the organisation?
- How much input will you have?
- How much group work will you do?

Larger groups need larger facilitation options. If you have a two-day event you might have to plan a sleep-over. You might need a microphone for people to give their views. If there is lots of group work you will need break-away spaces.

You need to clarify the terms of reference for the planning team that has been put in charge of the process. You must ensure that you have a full mandate from all sectors of your organisation.

An often neglected part of the strategic planning process is to make sure you have the necessary resources – people and financial – to make the process a success. If you have a great plan on paper, but no money to execute it, it will fail. This will frustrate members of your organisation and the next time you want to involve them in a strategic planning process they might not be interested.

Logistics and communication are an important part of strategic planning. You need to ensure that someone in your planning team is responsible for logistics, especially if your organisation serves a diverse community. For example, if you have a day-long meeting, ensure that you have catered for those in the group that might be vegetarian or who eat only food that is halaal.

Use the tools and techniques from project management to plan your strategic process; allocate responsibilities to different members of the planning team and assign deadlines to each team member.

If you do not spend enough time getting organised, a number of problems can arise and the whole process might fail.

7. 2. Analyse the situation

7.2.1. External environment

You need to consider these changing dynamics in the outside world:

- The political environment;
- The economic environment;
- The social environment;
- The technological environment;

- Demographics of your community;
- Legal changes;
- The people you serve – who are they and why do they need your services? and
- The broad needs of the community?

Remember that even if nothing in particular has changed, that is also an important point to note.

It also is useful to assign responsibility to different people in the organisation to do research. When you are discussing the external environment in the strategic planning process you will not only be going on the perceptions of the people in the room. You will be drawing also on objective information sources like newspapers, journals, books and other sources.

You also might invite external speakers to address you on various aspects. It is not necessary to research each area in depth, but you should focus on the areas that will have an impact on your organisation. For example, in a year of local government elections it is important to consider how the ward councillor might influence your community and what implications that might have for your organisation.

Use whatever technology you have at your disposal to get information and to get your message across.

7.2.2. Internal environment

It is important to remember the history, facts and origins of your organisation when you consider the internal environment of the organisation. Sometimes people who are part of the strategic planning process are not familiar with these aspects. They might frustrate the process because you have to keep going back to remind them of the various aspects of your history.

This might be boring for the people who know the history and facts of the organisation well because they have been there for a long time or their position in the organisation requires that they have this knowledge. If this is the case, you can have a lot fun by using creative

activities, such as role play or drawing cartoons or comics of the history of the organisation and getting people to share stories with one another.

At this point you have a choice ....you can either re-examine the vision, mission and values of your organisation or you can conduct a SWOT (strength, weaknesses, opportunities or threats) analysis.

Some organisations prefer to do a SWOT analysis

before they re-examine the vision, mission and values, while others prefer to do it the other way round so that their SWOT analysis is informed by these key documents.

There is not a right or a wrong way; it is simply a matter of preference. In this notebook we will examine the mission, vision and values first and what you should do during a strategic planning process. Then we will examine SWOT analysis in depth.

7.2.2.1. Vision

Vision encompasses the hopes and the dreams of your organisation. In fact, once your mission has been achieved as an organisation you will have achieved your vision. It is a description of a desirable future situation for the users of the organisation.

In essence your vision answers the question – What will it look like and what will we have achieved when we have been successful?

The statement that you come up with should be short and easy to communicate. It must be understood throughout the whole organisation. It must also be broad enough to last for a long time.

In every country the Constitution is the expression of that nation's vision for how it would like to be. It is an ideal that the people of that country strive for.

When deciding on your organisation's vision, try to get ideas and suggestions from as many people as possible. Your organisation's vision should be an inspiration to both the members of the organisation and people outside it.

When developing a vision you should consider the future and think about where your organisation will be in five or ten years.

A practical tip: try not to get a large group to write the vision. Rather ask one or two people to gather ideas and then draw up draft visions for the rest of the organisation to examine. Of course you will not please everyone, but you should try to develop a statement that includes all the ideas given to you.

For example:

VISION
GEM Youth Organisation
The youth of our community will be employable and will give back to their community through service

7.2.2.2. Mission

The mission statement explains to the world what it is that your organisation does. When outsiders read your mission statement, they will know why your organisation exists and how you hope to achieve your objectives.

Your mission statement should include your organisation's purpose and explain its core business. For example, if your organisation is working to decrease the prevalence of HIV/AIDS among 18-25 year olds, it would do so through public awareness campaigns, by encouring access to free testing and counselling and by helping young people in the community to gain access to antiretroviral medication through clinics.

You might have difficulty deciding on the wording of your mission statement, but even if the process is frustrating, you must ensure you reach agreement.

It is this statement that will inform your daily decision-making. It will help you to ensure that your organisation is successful. Regular evaluation or monitoring exercises will keep you on the right track.

MISSION
GEM Youth Organisation
To make young people employable we will provide life skills and business skills through youth service programmes run in community

7.2.2.3. Values statement

It is important to draw up a values statement for your CBO because it will enable outsiders to understand clearly how you operate and why you choose to do certain activities in a particular way.

A value is an underlying belief that we as individuals have. When you hear someone say, 'To me, honesty is the most important thing', that is his/her number one value. Your CBO's values statement should match irs vision and mission statements. These values inform every aspect of your organisation, from recruiting, to management and to how you make financial decisions.

It might not be enough to simply draw up a list of values. You might need to write a paragraph or two on what each value means to the organisation.

VALUES STATEMENT
GEM Youth Organisation
We are a youth-centered, democratic and empowered organisation that strives to improve our community through co-operation, knowledge-sharing and transparent communication.

7.2.2.4. SWOT analysis

SWOT stands for strengths, weaknesses, opportunities and threats. In this part of strategic planning it is vital to try to be as honest and critical as possible about your organisation.

It also is important to remember that often people tend to focus only on the weaknesses and threats, because they believe these need to be 'fixed'. However, vital issues can be missed if you do not focus on the positive aspects of your organisation too. Ask yourself: what should we do to keep doing the things we do well?

Opportunities often represent new avenues of work and growth for organisations, so you should spend substantial time focusing on this area.

Strengths and weaknesses refer to issues inside your organisation. Opportunities and threats relate to issues that are external to the organisation.

When you analyse your organisation and its business, it's often a good idea to hold group discussions. Allow people to brainstorm. List and categorise the issues under debate. Don't try to 'fix' everything. Choose the issues carefully and decide on the five most important ones. A good guideline is to choose five issues under each SWOT heading, ie five issues under strengths, five under weaknesses, five under opportunities and five under threats.

You need to decide what issues should be given priority. One way of doing this is to allow each delegate to vote for each issue. Assign points, for example each delegate might have four votes – the first vote is 6 points, the second vote is 4 points, the third vote is 2 points and the last vote is 1 point. Once you add up all the numbers, you will see which issues are the most important and which you need to focus on first.

GEM YOUTH ORGANISATION SWOT ANALYSIS

Strengths	Weaknesses
✧ Commitment (22) ✧ Enthusiasm in community (27) ✧ Good networks (14) ✧ Office space (25) ✧ Donated equipment (26) ✧ Well-trained facilitators (26)	✧ Not very old organisation (14) ✧ Conflict (30) ✧ Communication (25) ✧ Lack of funding (40)
Opportunities	**Threats**
✧ Youth Service on the increase in South Africa (30) ✧ No other youth organisations in our community (12) ✧ Lots of young people – we can choose the best (15) ✧ Funding from Umsobomvu Youth Fund (40)	✧ Commitment of young people if no money (30) ✧ Young people get jobs during programme (12) ✧ Facilitators move to other youth service programmes (25)

You are now ready to begin identifying the strategies that you need to employ to address the SWOT priorities.

7.3. Developing a strategy

You should now take each priority issue and develop a strategy to address it. Ideally you should come up with a number of strategies for each issue. This way you can choose the best strategy to follow within the context of your CBO's skills and resources.

Decide on the best strategy for your organisation and focus your resources on this particular approach. Don't try to focus on all strategies.

Later you might find that the strategy you have decided on is not working. You can always go back and look at the alternative strategies you had identified.

If, for example, one of the critical issues facing your organisation is a lack of financial resources. The strategies available to you might include:

- Talk to present funders to increase your funding
- Find new funders
- Start income-generating projects
- Tender for local government contracts

In developing your strategies you should ask the following questions:

- What are we trying to achieve?
- Why do need to achieve this?
- What do we need to achieve this?
- How will we go about achieving this?
- What skills and resources will we need to achieve this?

Each strategy should have goals and objectives to inform your plan. Once you have identified all of the above you are ready to develop a proper planning document.

7.4. Draft a plan

The planning document is important because it will guide the future of the organisation. You should use all the information available to you.

The planning document can be useful when you approach prospective funders. It shows them that your CBO is informed, aware of what is needed in the community and that it is committed to making the necessary changes to ensure its survival and growth.

You should include the following:

- Internal and external analysis;

- Vision, mission and values statements;
- SWOT analysis;
- Priority issues; and
- Proposed strategies.

This part of the process is usually the most detailed. It's best to form a small team of people, each of whom can write different sections of the document.

Remember to allocate timelines to each strategy. Make sure one person is the 'caretaker' and is responsible for each strategy. Think about the resources it will take to achieve the strategy.

For example, if you have chosen income generation as a strategy to alleviate your financial situation, think about where you will get start-up capital; decide which people will be responsible for this; and set up a budget because it costs money to make money.

Once you have written the first draft of your strategic plan document, you should circulate it for approval. Some people might recommend changes. Once these have been made, the strategic planning team should make a final submission.

7.5. Approve the plan

It seems obvious to point out that you should get approval of the plan from all the relevant structures in the organisation, such as the board.

Without approval, you will not have the commitment and buy-in of all the parties involved and conflict could arise. Once the plan is approved the hard work begins. Now you have to ensure the plan gets implemented.

7.6. Implement the plan

The first step in implementing the plan is to ensure that you have informed all the relevant people involved. You might have to hold meetings, give presentations or hand out copies of the plan to everyone. If your CBO has e-mail facilities, you can send everyone in the organisation a copy of the plan. You could put up posters reminding everyone of the organisation's strategic choices. Once the planning process is over people get on with their everyday activities and can forget about the forward-looking strategies that you have put in place.

To ensure this does not happen, you should give one or two people overall responsibility for the implementation of the plan. They should have the support of senior members of the organisation. These people should be the drivers of the strategic car that must be kept moving forward. The strategic car should go into reverse only when it is clear that one of the strategies chosen is not working.

At least one person should take responsibility for each activity in the strategic plan. Set deadlines for each activity. When the deadline is close, ensure that the person responsible is on track. Motivate and monitor the work. Ensure that those responsible know that a report on the work will be delivered at the board meeting. Everyone must be informed that they need to take their tasks seriously.

You might do a yearly review of your plan to ensure you are still on track.

7.7. Monitoring and evaluating the plan

One person should be appointed to be responsible for overall monitoring and evaluation of the plan. Whoever is chosen should have sufficient authority to ensure that the tasks are being implemented. S/he will be held accountable by the board for the successful implementation of the plan.

Think about the following key questions when you are monitoring and evaluating the implementation of the plan:

Are goals and objectives being achieved or not? If they are, then acknowledge, reward and communicate the progress. If not, then consider the following questions.

- Will the goals be achieved according to the timelines specified in the plan? If not, why not?
- Should the deadlines for completion be changed (be careful about making these changes – know why tasks are behind schedule before times are changed)?
- Do staff/volunteers have adequate resources (money, equipment, facilities, training, etc) to achieve the goals?
- Are the goals and objectives still realistic?
- Should priorities be changed to focus more on achieving the goals?
- Should the goals be changed (be careful about making these changes – know why the goals are not being achieved before changing them)?
- What can be learnt from the monitoring and evaluation to improve future planning activities and also to improve future monitoring and evaluation efforts?

Questions adapted from Carter MacNamara (MAP for Non-Profits)

Record changes to the strategic plan constantly. Keep the original copies of the plan so that you can track what worked and what did not. It is important to celebrate the achievement of tasks and strategies and to acknowledge the individuals responsible. This will encourage people to participate in future and to realise there is a purpose to strategic planning.

8. Conclusion

The strategic planning process has a number of key steps, all of which require preparation, careful thought, good facilitation and a commitment to execution and follow-up work.

Strategic planning is not a once-off event – it is a process that takes place over time, sometimes as long as three to five year. Simply drafting and drawing up the plan can take up to a year if done thoroughly.

Don't be intimidated. Remember that the more efficient your preparation and the more thorough your analysis, the better your plan will be.

The preparation will determine the outcome and will make it easier to achieve all the steps in the plan.

Strategic planning will ensure your organisation grows from strength to strength.

9. References

Books

1992. DPSU *Number One – Resource Booklet Series: Strategic Planning for Civics: A Workshop hosted by the Civic Association of Johannesburg and the Urban Foundation.* Development Strategy & Policy Unit Publications. Johannesburg

1992. DPSU. *Number Two – Resource Booklet Series: Strategic Planning for Civics: A workshop hosted by SANCO (Southern*

Natal) and the Urban Foundation. Development Strategy & Policy Unit Publications. Johannesburg.

1997. Thaw, Davine. How well do your 'read' your organisation? *Organisation Diagnosis in Ideas for Change Part 2* – December. Olive publications. Durban.

Manuals

2004. Idasa. *Mission, Vision & Values.*

Websites

26 August 2005. 'http://www.idasa.org.za' www.idasa.org.za

26 August 2005. 'http://www.mapfornonprofits.org' www.mapfornonprofits.org

27 August 2005. 'http://www.des.calstate.edu' www.des.calstate.edu

27 August 2005. 'http://www.allianceonline.org' www.allianceonline.org

28 August 2005. 'http://www.idealist.org' www.idealist.org

www.ingramcontent.com/pod-product-compliance
Lightning Source LLC
Chambersburg PA
CBHW072130020426
42334CB00018B/1738

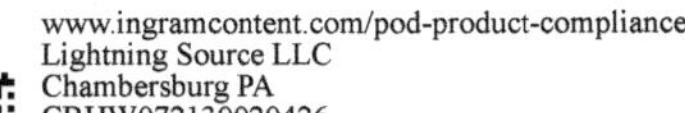

* 9 7 8 1 9 2 0 1 1 8 4 8 8 *